THE
GRIEF SURVIVAL
HANDBOOK

A GUIDE FROM HEARTACHE TO HEALING

D. KEITH COBB, M.D.

All information and comments are intended for general medical information only. For specific diagnosis and treatment of any medical conditions, please consult your personal physician.

Order this book online at www.trafford.com
or email orders@trafford.com

Most Trafford titles are also available at major online book retailers.

Print information available on the last page.

ISBN: 978-1-4120-8571-7 (sc)
ISBN: 978-1-4269-4122-1 (e)

Library of Congress Control Number: 2009936089

Because of the dynamic nature of the Internet, any web addresses or links contained in this book may have changed since publication and may no longer be valid. The views expressed in this work are solely those of the author and do not necessarily reflect the views of the publisher, and the publisher hereby disclaims any responsibility for them.

Any people depicted in stock imagery provided by Getty Images are models, and such images are being used for illustrative purposes only.
Certain stock imagery © Getty Images.

Trafford rev. 06/17/2020

 www.trafford.com

North America & international
toll-free: 1 888 232 4444 (USA & Canada)
fax: 812 355 4082

In memory of
Dan and Jewel Waller
O.W. and Inez Cobb

CONTENTS

ACKNOWLEDGEMENTS

I am indebted to my editor, Dr. Nancy Remler, for her
patient literary guidance.

Kind thanks to my encouraging wife, Amy,
who serves as my reviewer
for this and other publications.

I am most grateful to those who have shared the stories
herein and in doing so
have been my mentors.

Introduction

"In grief, nothing stays put.
One keeps emerging from a phase, but it always recurs.
Round and round. Everything repeats.
Am I going in circles, or dare I hope I am on a spiral?
But if I spiral, am I going up or down it?"
-C.S. Lewis

OF ALL EXPERIENCES known to man, mourning is one of the most difficult to encounter. It is a time of deep despair that is difficult to place into words. Unless one has been through that dark time, it is impossible to fully imagine the array of emotions that accompany the grief. Disbelief, shock, anger, fear, hopelessness, and a profound sense of loss are unwelcome companions to the mourner.

When tragedy strikes us, these emotions change our lives dramatically. We feel as if our life has been shattered beyond repair. It becomes difficult to imagine what a normal day was like, and it seems unlikely that life will ever be normal again.

"Survivors include" is a common phrase in an obituary that conveys more than just the names of those still living. For in many instances those left to carry on with life feel as if that is just what they are doing – surviving. Yet, as impossible as it may seem, somehow we find a way to endure this complicated and dreaded era in our lives.

A crucial aspect of the healing process involves a simple yet difficult task – that of gradually accepting the pain of grief. It will be an inescapable period of time littered with hurt and anguish. Tolerating the unpleasantness of grief may be a more reasonable goal for us at first, but eventually acceptance can occur. Just how long this time of tolerating the pain will last is impossible to predict. It may take a few weeks or it may take years.

Tolerating and eventually accepting the pain does not necessarily make the process less traumatic and less painful. However, it does help us realize that the overwhelming emotions, the vague physical symptoms and the spiritual bleakness are all normal encounters of mourners. And it helps us incrementally move toward healing.

Simply knowing that these emotional encounters are to be expected may keep us from thinking we are going insane (a common thought among mourners) or are psychologically less stable than we once considered ourselves. Grief can be a very humbling experience. Yet with humility comes the open door of accepting the grace of friends, family and faith. All are important resources for each of us.

And as we accept the pain we can then allow ourselves the restoration that occurs as we travel this arduous journey of mourning. At some point we can enjoy good memories of loved ones without concomitant pain and tears. One day we can joyfully appreciate and recall the laughter and camaraderie without searing loneliness accompanying each recollection.

In the following pages, I hope you will find some insight into this difficult emotional road that none of us wish to travel but will. Whether we are princes or paupers, grief affects us all; it does not respect position, prosperity or poverty. It pays an uninvited visit to each of us at some point in our lives. And when it does, it brings more than overnight luggage. In fact, the emotional baggage which grief brings may be with us for years to come. Even though grief may live with us for a while, it does not have to rule the house - at least not forever.

Unless people experience grief firsthand, they cannot truly understand the crisis a grieving individual experiences. Those who have walked this difficult path are the ones to give the best advice and words of comfort. Over the years of seeing many of my patients and my own family survive grief, I am repeatedly amazed at the resilience that eventually emerges. Some individuals are just beginning their mourning while others have been experiencing it for years and are just coming to grips with the death of their loved ones. I have often asked how they cope with their tremendous losses.

Those you will read about have been generous enough to permit me to recount their grief experiences. As requested, some names and minor situational details have been changed to protect privacy. But all are true stories of deep hurt eventually followed by gradual healing. It is their desire that you will find hope and comfort in reading of their struggles and how they overcame their grief.

Most of these stories relate to the death of a family member, but some tell of the fallout from divorce or abuse. In either circumstance, the pain and disorientation is overbearing. But it is ultimately survivable.

Like you, tragedy has come to my family over the years and has taken a substantial toll. Yet I have also seen friends and family display great determination and strength and gradually come to terms with sorrow and manage to cultivate some good from life's rubbish pile.

During medical school, physicians must learn a wide spectrum of diseases and treatments. While professors and textbooks attempt to teach about the process of death and dying, the patients, our families and even grief itself often teaches us more. Not all people heal in textbook fashion, either. After years of revisiting and re-reading many books and medical journals on the subject of grief, I suspect many well intended authors have not actually been through the burden of losing a child or spouse. Medical books often describe grief with a time frame of months, yet in the vast majority of my acquaintances, it lasts for years. And while there are common strategies to recovery, individual healing varies from person to person.

As a mourner (or as one helping a mourner) who reads these pages, may you find the strength to continue on this path of bereavement, knowing that the only way to reach its end is not by living above or around the grief, but by living *through* it.

It will by no means be an easy task, but you can, and indeed, you will survive this journey. Don't expect the hurt to go away in a few weeks, or even a few months. It will take much longer. Don't expect life to be the same as it was before your loss. Life will be different.

You will likely live with some emotional scars. These scars may outlive the initial hurt and sorrow. Much like physical scars, emotional scars can intermittently pain us throughout our lifetime.

You can expect days of relapse into deep sorrow and even into self pity. One must be patient and willing - willing to put forth a significant amount of effort -willing to tolerate the pain - willing to heal. In fact at some point, you may need to go beyond being willing and become proactive in your healing. And don't be discouraged if every day or each week doesn't show signs of your healing.

Sometimes emotional setbacks may seem more frequent than the progress of healing. But even on the days when recovery seems impossible, you must allow it to occur - even if only in small increments. You can be assured that, in time, healing will occur.

CHAPTER ONE: "I NEVER HAVE"

*"The deep pain that is felt at the death of every friendly soul arises
from the feeling that there is in every individual something which is
inexpressible, peculiar to him alone, and is, therefore, absolutely and
irretrievably lost."*
Arthur Schopenhauer

INEZ WAS TWENTY-FOUR years old when her two year-old
son, Howell, was tragically burned in a house fire. For two
horrible days, the child lay in a hospital bed as his family
hoped and prayed that he would survive the major burns.
But after tearful hours of anguish, Howell died due to smoke
inhalation and lung damage.

His young parents were absolutely devastated beyond words.
How could their lives go on after such a profound loss? Would
their home and family ever be normal again? Would the unbearable pain ever subside?

Unfortunately, grief was no stranger to Inez, for when she was
only ten years old her own mom passed away. Grief called again
when she was in her seventies as one of her daughters, Ouida, was

diagnosed with a breast tumor and a few months later succumbed to the ravages of cancer.

Only a few years later, Inez became a widow after 51 years of marriage. She never remarried. She aged gracefully, without any display of bitterness over her losses. Near the end of her life, she felt as if she had lived happily and was blessed in spite of the tragedies she endured. This wonderful lady was my grandmother.

After I became a parent and my oldest daughter turned two, I was reminded of the untimely death of my grandmother's son when he was that same age. I wondered how anyone could endure the death of a child, especially one so young and innocent.

While my daughter, Carmen, and I were swinging with my grandmother on her front porch one spring day, reluctantly I asked my grandmother how she ever overcame the devastating loss. To my surprise, she smiled and said, "I never have".

In retrospect, the surprise was not the words she spoke, but rather the gentle manner in which she spoke them. I was concerned that my inquiry might bring up horrible memories and a quick, evasive answer. Yet she bravely described the terrible incident to me with sketchy details that were decades later filled in vividly when told to me by her daughter Bea.

Aunt Bea was 4 years old when her brother Howell died. Almost eighty years later she could still recall the incident as if it had happened yesterday. Her memories add the view of a child to the story my grandmother told me several years ago.

My aunt recalled her family moving from Georgia to Florida where they were living in the first floor of a two story apartment. It was a pleasant December day in 1924 as grandmother was washing the children's clothes in the back yard. Aunt Bea slipped across the street to play with her cousins while my grandmother, Howell and the baby, Ouida, were occupied with the laundry.

As two year-olds will do, Howell quietly slipped out of his mother's sight for a few minutes. He made his way to the second floor apartment to visit some of his extended family when a fire from a wood burning stove grew out of control. As the upstairs became engulfed in flames and smoke rolled out the windows, panic set in as my grandmother frantically looked for her son.

After a few seemingly eternal moments, my grandmother realized he was in the burning house. She rushed up the smoked filled stairs to hear Howell screaming in a room with a locked door. Grandmother broke down the entry door and entered a blaze filled room where she found her scorched and sobbing child crouched behind a bedroom door.

She rescued him from the inferno and rushed down the stairs, barely escaping death in doing so. After grandmother made her way out of the burning building, an ambulance soon arrived and carried her and Howell to a local emergency room as the firemen remained behind to douse the flames.

In spite of the best medical care of the 1920's, Howell died nine hours later due to smoke inhalation. Aunt Bea could still remember seeing her baby brother in their mother's arms after she rescued him. Seven decades later she recalled the smell of singed hair, clothing and flesh as well as the screams and the sirens of that horrible scene. For the rest of her life when she would learn of a childhood tragedy, it stirred unwanted, ghostly memories from her childhood. Undoubtedly, my grandmother experienced the same flashbacks.

Howell's funeral was held the day before Christmas Eve in 1924. My grandmother had already bought presents for her three children, including Howell. She later quietly opened his presents and placed them in a trunk, never to be played with by her son.

Aunt Bea remembered those special toys and how years later she and her sister would plead with her mother to let them play with them. But their mother would only allow them to look at those treasures from time to time and immediately would place them back in the trunk – much like placing them in a coffin.

Aunt's Bea's rendition of the story was actually more detailed than the one my grandmother told me years ago. Even though my grandmother had no doubt relived, replayed and retold herself the story repeatedly, the story told to me was brief and was free of the terror I felt when Aunt Bea spoke her version. I suspect grandmother was to the point in her life where telling the story in detail was not as important as was pointing out to me that overcoming a loss was possible.

When I first heard my grandmother tell of this tragedy, I could only imagine the bitter pain she must have felt back then, and even years later as she was sharing the details with me. I thought of my own two year-old daughter and wondered if and how I could ever overcome such a traumatic event such as the death of my own child. Hearing her story brought a visceral unpleasantness.

Yet my grandmother told it without a tremor in her voice or a tear in her eye. How could she endure such pain? How could she survive this loss? How did she live with the memories? How could she forgive herself for letting her son slip away to play, even if only for a few moments? I did not ask these hard questions, yet she could see I wanted to. "I never got over my loss," she said, "but I have learned to live with it."

Just how she did so, I never really understood. The grief I had experienced thus far at that point in my life seemed shallow compared to her burden. She did not offer to explain just how she accepted her loss, likely realizing that I would not fully comprehend.

Decades later when Aunt Bea filled in some of the details of the story, I learned that for many years my grandmother blamed herself for the death of her child. She struggled profoundly to overcome her devastation. Her statement that she "learned to live with it" greatly oversimplified decades of grief and self-blame. But over the years, it appeared that somehow she learned to do so.

My grandmother is no longer with us, but my memories of her are not of a bitter, grieving person. Rather, I remember her kindness and her keen dry humor. Memories of her loss never completely left her, yet she laughed again. She smiled again. She loved again, perhaps more than she would have without her loss.

She was not a person of wealth, yet was generous with all she owned. She and her husband reared seven other wonderful children. She was a devoutly religious woman whom I considered a saint, yet she would likely laugh off such a title for herself. Even though she experienced her share of tragedy, she went on to enjoy a long life which she described as blessed.

Christmas at her home was never for me a sad occasion. Although, that holiday must have been difficult for her throughout the remainder of her life, she was always joyous and hospitable at Christmastime. Were it not for Aunt Bea's details, I would never have suspected Christmas was a complex time of grief memories for my grandmother.

She never allowed me to see much of her grief. I do recall her mourning when Papa Cobb passed away. The day after he died I went to her home and found her in the kitchen preparing food for the many family members who were returning home to attend to the funeral. She stood in front of her stove as the smell of a home cooked meal lingered in the air.

As I made my way past my aunts who were busily helping in the kitchen I had no idea what to say to my grandmother to bring her comfort. "I'm sorry" was all I could muster. Her reply was a very long embrace that only a grandmother can give and the whispered words, "I'll be all right". I think surviving would be an accurate description of how we all were doing that day.

My grandmother never fully explained to me how she survived her tragedy, but as you will read in the next chapter I suspect she did so in much the same fashion as my mother's parents did several years later.

Chapter Two:
The Death of an Adult Child

"If you are going through hell, keep going."
- Winston Churchill

MY OTHER GRANDPARENTS also experienced the death of a son, but their son was an adult who had just become a father himself when he died. Bill was their youngest son, who had only been married two years. He experienced the joy of fatherhood only thirteen months before a tragic automobile accident took his life. He was not killed at the time of the wreck, but after several weeks of lying unconscious in a hospital bed, he died on his 25th birthday. His wife, Norma, survived the crash.

Forty years later, I can still recall my nauseous emotions that accompanied the news of Uncle Bill's death. It is an emotional reaction to the news of death or tragedy to which we never grow accustomed. Even more so, I remember sensing the emotional devastation of my grandparents, my parents and Aunt Norma.

For the remainder of my grandparent's lives any reminder of Bill's accident was painful.

During the first few years after the accident I would occasionally hear my grandmother in her bedroom trying to muffle her sobs as she struggled to survive her mournful anguish. My grandfather would quietly assure me that she would be alright after a good cry. For the rest of her life she was easily distraught upon hearing news of car accidents, sirens and even upon the sight of an ambulance. Almost half a century later, my grandparents would at times become tearful when they talked of Bill.

Eventually, my grandparents came to a point where they could enjoy talking about good times with Bill. In fact, it seemed to especially help my grandmother when we talked of him. My grandparents had a special place in their heart for Bill's son and took much pride in his accomplishments. Seeing him grow into a successful young man seemed to give my grandparents some consolation at losing their own son.

At age 89, my grandfather (whom I called Dandaddy) told me of the days and months following the death of his son over five decades prior. "It took something out of me - something I don't think I ever really got back," he said. It was as if a portion of his own life died along with his son.

When asked how he overcame the grief, he credited his family, his faith and his church for helping him through that time. Staying busy with his work and grandkids kept his mind occupied and was to some extent a distraction from the grief; yet no amount of activity could alleviate the painful gloom. Since his own children were grown and no longer lived at home with my grandparents, Dandaddy made a conscious effort to spend more time with his grandchildren, as did my grandmother.

As the years passed, I came to regard my grandfather more and more as a friend, as well as a grandparent. The numerous hours we spent at his home, on his farm just outside the small town where he lived, horseback riding, fishing and doing many other activities together, provided me with a treasured relationship which I experienced from childhood into adulthood.

When I was a child, my grandparents would often drive from the nearby town where they lived to pick my brother and me up after school on Friday. During the weekends we spent with them, we took rides on country roads, visited relatives, cooked together, picked vegetables and at night went to the local burger shop for dinner. But more than the specifics of *what* we did, I remember we did *something* and did it together frequently.

Frequently, Dandaddy would do something special as I sat beside him on his sofa. As we talked (and sometimes when we were quiet), he held my hand. He not only did this when I was a child, but even when I was an adult. In fact, he would do so with his other grandchildren and great-grandchildren as well. Sitting and talking while my elderly grandfather held my hand is something I still fondly remember as a gesture of his gentleness and of his love for me. I have often wondered if he had an enhanced insight into life's fragility and had learned to hold tight to those around him.

Dandaddy lost his wife, Jewel, to Alzheimer's disease about ten years before he died. The night she died, my grandfather and I held each other and cried. Then he whispered the same words I had heard many years earlier from my other grandmother that sad day of mourning in her kitchen, "I'll be all right".

In my earliest memories of my grandfather I recall the excitement and anticipation while riding in his truck as we drove to his farm on the outskirts of the small town where he lived. As a young child, the thrill of these frequent weekend jaunts culminated as we turned off the highway and onto an unpaved county road where without a word spoken between us, I would slip across the blue vinyl bench seat and into my grandfather's lap to drive. At that young age, my legs could not reach the accelerator, brake or clutch, so with practice we became a driving team. With his prompting and pressing the clutch, I would proudly change the gears as we rattled down the bumpy Georgia clay roads.

It took a few years, but one day I noticed that my grandfather was covertly placing one of his hands onto the left lower portion of steering wheel to keep us between the ditches and at that moment I realized he had done so for quite some time. For the next year or so, the challenge became to drive well enough so as to have him leave the actual steering to me. As I grew and my boyhood legs lengthened enough to allow me to reach the pedals on the floor board (at least when sitting on the front edge of the seat), he soon cautiously and not without much begging on my part took the passenger seat. He gently chided my grinding of the gears and laughed when I strained both our necks from accelerating too quickly.

In the months after Bill died, my grandfather and I continued the regular weekend rides in the country but he was quieter and more contemplative than I was accustomed to, but the profound devastation I noted in the days after Bill's death was not evident. He did not even seem overly depressed to me. We still found things to laugh about. We continued to fish and ride horses together. Life continued on and he appeared intent on keeping his own grief from adversely affecting his relationship with me.

For the next forty years we would intermittently maintain those ritualistic rides to his farm. After entering adulthood, the novel thrill of driving his truck had passed so I usually was the passenger as we drove past summer fields of green corn and soybeans and autumn acres of white cotton. We discussed the timing of fertilizer application and when to cut timber. He often recalled his family's stuggle during the Great Depression and how fortunate he was to have found a good job and to eventually buy a farm. We talked of raising children, the importance of saving money and other grandfatherly advice gently sprinkled in the conversation between more often mentioned topics such as the weather and the livestock.

A few months before his death, my ninety-year-old grandfather reluctantly gave up driving, so he became the passenger again on our weekend rides. Knowing he was approaching the end of life, he became quiet again, much the way he was after his son's death. He had recently insisted on moving into a local nursing home and politely refused to move in with any of his family. On a cool winter afternoon while on those same bumpy roads where he taught me to change gears, I asked him if he was becoming depressed. He reflected for a moment while looking out the passenger window and replied, "We all have to adjust and accept things". And then he added with a tear in his eye, "We've had some good times on these roads together". My mind was suddenly flooded with memories of sitting in his lap as a child and steering his truck down this same lane. I quietly agreed while trying to see the road ahead through my own tears knowing that this brief afternoon ride to the farm would be one of our last. Indeed it was and just a few weeks later my grandfather died.

Our frequent drives from his home to his farm were only a few, short miles, but the recollections of riding with the windows down in his pick-up are long-lived. Of course, there were many other important events I shared with my grandfather but the late afternoons riding with him in his truck exemplify my memories of him.

My grandparents lost something irreplaceable when they lost their son. But they took that loss and made a commitment to emotionally invest in the lives of their family, especially their children and grandchildren. By focusing on those with whom they were still able to love and influence, they took an irretrievable loss and made it an indispensable gain for others.

Did such pain and anguish make them better people? Did their depression, suffering and regrets eventually and mysteriously improve their lives? I don't know the answer to those deep questions, but I strongly suspect that their *response* to their tragedy eventually contributed to making *me* a better person. And if one of, if not the highest, aspirations in life is to bring charity, mercy and encouragement into the lives of others, my grandparents accomplished that well. And it came out of their tragedy.

CHAPTER THREE:
THE GRIEF OF MISCARRIAGE

"Give sorrow words; the grief that does not speak
Whispers the o'er fraught heart and bids it break."
- William Shakespeare

PARENTS OF STILLBORN infants and miscarried babies grieve deeply over their loss, more so than most persons realize. It is often the mother who carries much of the grief since she will usually feel more attached to the child inside her womb than does the father. Her profound emotional attachment is augmented by a very real physical connection as she forms an elaborate system of sharing nutrients and oxygen with her baby via the umbilical cord.

After our second anniversary, my wife, Amy, and I unexpectedly found ourselves expecting a child. Although somewhat surprised by the news, we were looking forward to becoming parents. But during the first trimester, Amy experienced physical signs that the pregnancy was not going well. After a call to her obstetrician, she was placed on bed-rest. But bed rest, hopes and prayer were not enough to prevent the loss of the child a few days later. It was a painful and somewhat bewildering time for me, but much more so for Amy.

Mothers who lose a baby to miscarriage experience grief compounded by the fact that there is no wake or funeral where friends and family can express sympathy and support and can acknowledge the life that was lost. There is no grave stone to mark the burial site or memorialize the child's brief existence.

People often innocently comment in an ineffective effort to console, offering such well-intended remarks as, "You'll have another baby" or "At least it happened early in the pregnancy." In reality having another baby is not the issue. The miscarried baby is the one the mother wanted. And early or late in pregnancy is not the issue since there is no good time to lose the child inside.

Women who miscarry (and their families and friends) often do not know if they really should consider themselves mothers at all. They wonder if they conceive but do not deliver, does that count as motherhood? They also question if something is wrong with their bodies and if they will ever be able to carry a child to delivery. The losses of self-confidence, of trust in life and of optimism toward the future are frequent consequences of miscarriage. The mother's basic identity may be lost. She may feel inadequate, even embarrassed at her inability to carry the child.

Miscarriage Support Auckland offers the following insight:

> Miscarriage involves a number of potential significant losses and is a complex grief that can involve an additional kind of suffering that is not necessarily present with other types of bereavement. Not only have we lost our baby, we are suffering from the effects of a birth and a death and we usually do not have a baby to bury. A funeral normally gives others their cue of how to behave appropriately and where there isn't one they are often at

a loss themselves and may not even realize we are grieving. This adds to our stress as we can then feel we need to explain this, whereas with a still-born birth or loss of a child, everyone is aware of the devastation and expects to grieve. People may not want to talk about what has happened, and it's the only thing we can think of.

When our miscarriage has been early in the pregnancy (or even later) it can be minimized and invalidated, but for us, it is the strength of the bond with our baby not the length of the pregnancy that determines the depth of our grief.

An obstetrician who loses his (or her) child in a miscarriage will find the chilling reminder of their loss delivered along with each newborn. Obstetric sonographers will find it difficult to return to work and ultrasound images of unborn children kicking and grasping in the womb. Seeing the joy of an expectant mother watching her baby's heart beat on the ultrasound display screen only serves to remind the sonographer that her child's heart stopped beating and in the process her own heart was broken.

The first few years after losing a child, mothers and fathers are in a precarious period. Women who miscarry experience this dangerous period more than men. This was true in our miscarriage. While I felt sad, disillusioned and confused for many weeks, Amy's emotions went beyond such and left her with significant grief for a much longer time. And while miscarriage presents a significant emotional drain, parents who experience the death of a living child have an increased risk of automobile accidents and even suicide for the first few years after losing their child. Of course, suicide only makes things worse for the surviving spouse and siblings.

Most mothers have a longer grieving period than fathers and more health problems associated with grieving, perhaps because they are more involved with the day to day care of the child. The mother's daily routine and purpose in life is tragically altered. This is not to say that a father's grief and pain are, or are not, any less than a mother's, but it seems to take longer for the mom's grief to resolve. Such a long grieving period and the associated health risks can even shorten a person's life, especially if the grief is not responded to appropriately. Losing a child is one of the most extreme stressors a person might experience. It is worsened when it happens unexpectedly from a tragedy. But as you have and will read, it is something that can be survived.

CHAPTER FOUR:
THE GRIEVING CHILD

*"Sorrow makes us all children again – destroys all differences of intellect.
The wisest know nothing."*
-Ralph Waldo Emerson

I WAS SEVEN years old when my mother's younger brother was killed in the tragic automobile accident described in Chapter Two. Four decades later I still recall the disconcerting emotions of that time. I remember the night my mother answered the phone and within a few minutes we were packing suitcases and loading the car to make the drive to the hospital.

After Uncle Bill died, I remember contemplating death and wondering what happens to us when we die. I wondered if he knew he was in a casket. Did he know how much his family longed for him? Did he know how much my grandmother cried for him? Then I realized that one day, I too would die. What would death be like for me? What if I was very sick and everyone thought I had died? What would happen if I were buried alive?

Such questions and concerns are common among children as they learn about death and dying. Yet they are often reluctant to share these thoughts with others.

The news of death brought feelings of sadness, fear and repulsion. It was my first experience with that terrible nauseous feeling that accompanies bad news. I was very uncomfortable being around my extended family in the days following the death, as I did not know what to say nor how to act in response to my family's devastating loss. Such loss of direction is not unique to children, but is experienced by adults as well, especially during one's first exposure to death and grief.

Only a few generations ago, children more closely observed death in what was then a largely rural based economy. Those reared on family farms saw the births and deaths of farm animals as well as the home births of siblings. Home stillbirths were not uncommon. Occasionally families would experience deaths of family members who lived at home with them, such as elderly grandparents. The bodies were usually prepared in the homes for burial. In areas without funeral directors, families and community members would come to the residence of the deceased to clean, dress and place the body in a casket.

My dad's mother recalled being a child when her mother died of cancer. She peeped through the kitchen door to watch female relatives and neighbors who had gathered in the kitchen after the death of her mother. The body rested on the kitchen table where the ladies prepared her mother for burial. As was common in the early 1900's, the funeral wake was held overnight in the home with an open casket viewing provided for the family and friends.

The dying process in our country changed in the last half of the twentieth century and subsequently the manner in which we experience death and dying. Although modern hospice programs allow many patients the opportunity to die at home, most deaths now occur in either a hospital or a nursing home. Funeral homes professionally provide for the preparation of the deceased. Most children and many adults are somewhat removed from the dying process and from the actual death itself.

As with adults, grief in childhood is a journey, not just an illness which can be easily treated and cured. Children may carry their grief for many years. The psychic scar will heal and cover the emotional wound, but likely there will always be reminders of their loss.

Children's grief responses vary according to age and past experience with death. Those aged two and under usually display a type of separation anxiety, much the same way infants react the first few times their mothers are away from them for more than just a few minutes. Crying, biting, hitting and sleep disturbances are common as children adjust to new care givers and to new routines in their daily lives.

Preschoolers aged three to five may regress in areas such as potty training, thumb sucking and avoiding others. Children may play out the scenes of the events leading to the deaths of parents or other family members. For instance, if a parent was killed in a car crash, the child may play out the death by pretending to wreck a car. Such play is normal and helps the child comprehend the death. Children may play out the tragedy rather than talk about it.

Children aged six to twelve may also play out the events of death, but are much more cognitively aware of the changes in their lives due to the deaths of family members. The first experience with grief is disturbing at any time of life, but when it occurs during childhood, it is especially confusing.

Children's pain from loss is just as real as that of adults, even though they may not understand all the ramifications of the loss at the time. Children will have many questions, most of them unspoken, concerning their future family roles. Children may also wonder how and if their family will continue to function as a unit.

It is important to be honest with children. Do not tell them that Dad is asleep and will come back one day. This dishonesty may cause them to persistently deny that a death has occurred and may foster mistrust. They may doubt your ability to be honest when they realize you did not tell them the truth. While it may be appropriate to explain to toddlers that death is like a prolonged sleep, we should not give them false hope that the deceased will be coming back. Even a four or five year-old can grasp the concept that death is more than a just slumber, and in time the child can comprehend that it is irreversible.

Children grieve at levels appropriate not only to their ages, but also commensurate to their stages of emotional development. For instance, an infant's separation anxiety may be soothed in a matter of days or weeks by another family member. Conversely, the adolescent will not so quickly find solace from the sympathy of the surviving parent or other family member. Grief is proportional to the ability to love, bond and to remember. These abilities take time to develop during childhood and thus the ability to grieve and the depth of mourning grows as a child matures.

When infants lose parents to death, as they grow they will long to learn more about the deceased parents. Asking questions about the deceased parents is healthy and helps children identify with the parents. The pain of grief may or may not be as intense for infants as it is for older children or adults, but infants' sense of longing for parents will persist for years. Infancy probably does protect children from some of the grievous pain, especially pain derived from memories of loved ones with which older children and adults must deal. However, as children grow, they will try to develop memories of deceased parents through pictures as well as family members' and friends' descriptions. This is a normal and healthy part of children's mourning processes.

Children of all ages may develop a strong over-dependence on the surviving parent. They may refuse to sleep in their own beds or beg the surviving parent not to go to work. They may insist on having others perform tasks which they usually can do for themselves. Sometimes they will refuse to go to school or leave the house unless the parent accompanies them. Once arriving at school, they may become deathly ill, only to regain instant health the moment the parent returns to school to take them home early. Such scenarios suggest regression, which would not be considered abnormal under the circumstances. Still, the surviving parent must help the grieving children work through them.

Much patience and reassurance are required as grieving children go through this phase of their grief. It may be days or weeks before children are ready to return to school. At least a few days or more away from school likely will be in order during the acute phase of grief. But usually activities such as school will give children some distraction from the grief. The daily routine of life can help them adjust.

Use your own judgment as when to place children back into school or other activities. Expect some regressive behavior, such as repeatedly requesting that you pick them up early from school. You must consider whether to go to the school a few times when your children show regressive behavior. It may be appropriate to bring them home a couple of times if they appear ill, but once they are deemed healthy, at some point it would be better to leave them at school on such occasions.

There may be days when you must gently assure your children that you will pick them up from school at the appropriate time of the day and not a minute sooner. Even though you may feel guilty in doing so, to do otherwise will simply reinforce the regressive behavior. When to take up this stance will be up to your best judgment.

At the same time, be careful not to discount all ailments during the period of mourning as purely psychological. If there is any doubt concerning a physical ailment, a physician appointment would be in order. All age groups can experience physical illness due to the extreme stress of grief. Stress can exacerbate existing medical conditions and precipitate new medical problems.

You may second-guess many decisions you make with your children. Undoubtedly, all parents will make some occasional mistakes in child rearing in such tense times. Yet raising children must continue, even in the face of grief. Do the best you can. When you make mistakes, admit it to yourself (and if needed, to your child) then move on and determine not to repeat your errors.

Occasionally children will display overly independent attitudes after the death of a parent. For instance, a daughter may try to take on all the roles of her deceased mother. She may insist on doing all the cooking, cleaning of the home and care of younger children while resisting all assistance from other members of the family. When a father dies, his young son may feel as if he needs to quit school and find a job to support the family, even if he is actually too young to do so. He may begin to dress and groom himself in the same manner as his dad once did in order to become the man of the family. These well-intended actions are not in themselves harmful, unless they inappropriately distract rather than help cope with the grieving process. Such actions often accompany denial. Children may incorrectly feel that if they assume all the responsibilities of the deceased family member, then the family will not miss the deceased person quite as much and the burden of mourning will be relieved.

Children can deny a death just as adults do but may manifest their denial in a variety of different ways. Their denial may take the form of playing more than usual as if nothing tragic has occurred. They may talk of Dad coming home soon or of plans they had made with him. Like younger infants and toddlers, older children may regress in their developmental stages as well with tantrums or loss of toilet-training skills.

Teenagers can well comprehend the concept of death, but during these vital years of developing into adulthood, grief can be especially hard to bear. They often will hide their grief in order not to appear as weak. Teens are vulnerable to peer pressure and do not usually wish to be seen as vastly different from their peers. For this reason, they may show no signs of mourning when they are with their friends. Offering support and love to those of this age group may require more of a physical presence and the use of listening skills rather than reasoning skills in conversation.

Teens may become withdrawn, secluded and even angry in much the same manner as adults do when responding to death. They may find it difficult to draw closer to and to depend upon adults at a time in their development when they are finding their own identity and some degree of independence. Youth of all developmental stages will learn some, if not most, of their mourning behavior from their parents or other influential adults in their lives. When adults deal with grief in an appropriate and healthy manner, the children will likely do the same.

Children of all ages may express their grief though regressive behavior, violent outbursts, seclusion or similar personality changes during this time. More than explanations, they will need support of a listening companion who is willing to wait for the right moment when children allow themselves to open up and express their fears and hurt. This expression of grief will likely take place gradually as the children work through the different phases of grief. They will ask many unanswerable questions, but a willingness to admit our own lack of understanding in some of life's difficult situations helps build trust which is based on honesty.

We should not force children to express their grief. Rather, we should allow mourning children to talk about or play out death on their own timetables and on their own levels. It is not helpful to oversimplify death, nor is it advantageous to over-glamorize heaven. In doing so, we may send the wrong message that it would be better if they also were to die as soon as possible in order to be with their lost loved one.

Like adults, children may experience a sense of rage at their loss. It is often a bewildering agitation. Anger is a common emotion of grief that when overly suppressed can be harmful. Expressing our feelings of rage, anger, regret and other strong emotions is usually helpful if done appropriately. But it is not healthy to express these emotions in a manner that focuses the rage toward those who do not deserve such blame. While it is tempting and even common for us to vent our hostilities on the nearest relative or friend, this often results in more harm than good. When we unleash our hostilities on someone who is trying to help, we often say or do things that both we and the other person regret. While it may occasionally be good to "get things off our chests", adults and children alike should do so in a way that will not cause regret to us nor harm to the listener. Yet it is appropriate and helpful to admit and to talk about the resentment and anger we are experiencing.

Most adults at some time or another are guilty of inappropriately venting our emotions to others in spite of our maturity and experience in life. Children will have an even more difficult time in learning to control these outbursts, especially during the stressful time of mourning. Youth will often release some frustration and grief on family members inappropriately. In a forbearing and supportive manner we should patiently provide verbal encouragement and direction when children are ready to express their sentiments.

Parents and friends should tolerate outbursts to some extent, but they should strongly discourage any disrespectful words or actions. While it will be difficult to prevent every toddler's tantrum, adults should offer older children appropriate reasoning and guidance about respectful behavior toward others. The best way to encourage appropriate behavior is through grieving appropriately with them.

In the months after Uncle Bill died my weekend visits to my grandparents would usually include a drive to the town cemetery to visit his grave. I initially found this to be an uncomfortable experience as it would consistently bring my grandmother to tears, and I would have no idea how to comfort her. As the months passed she became more composed on those occasions and I became more aware of the profound loss she had encountered. For decades and until her death she continued her regular trips to visit her son's grave. Now that she and my grandfather are buried beside him, I continue that tradition with a glimpse of insight into her need to frequent the plot of a loved one.

When influential adults hide their own pain of mourning by putting on a "good face" and always being happy in the presence of grieving children, the children may feel confused. They may wonder why grief is so personally painful to them, yet the adults in their life seem unaffected by the death. While we do not want to pour all our grief out upon children, we should not hide it completely. As children see our grief expressed through tears and other signs of mourning, they learn that others share their sadness and pain with them. They learn to grieve appropriately to life's disasters by the loving encouragement and example set by the adults in their life who are willing to mourn with them.

Chapter Five:
Losing a Spouse

Even though I talk to you almost every day,
It's between sleep and wake, like a place in the clouds,
Only then it seems I can hear your voice
Calling back, calling my name aloud.

For months I talked to your headstone,
But never got an answer to Why.
Why you had to go, why I had to stay.
Why I continue to live, why you had to die?

So many questions still go unanswered, so
After quite some time I finally stopped asking
As I could never find just the right answer.
I finally accepted, there's no way to avoid the sting.

Even though I can't clearly hear you,
I still see you as plain as can be.
Whenever our son looks at me, I see your eyes.
When he smiles so bright, it's your grin I see.

He strolls up to meet me and to my surprise,
There you are again in the way he walks.
For years I've seen him grow, becoming more like you
And now he even sounds much the same when he talks.

Recently he told me how he could not make it,
Not without at least one of us here to carry on.
And oh, how terribly he misses you too,
But unbearable life would be if both of us were gone.

And suddenly, there was at least an answer
To one of many, many why's.
It's because of him that I remain
To love, to teach, to hold when he cries.

So here I stay with the ones left behind -
Missing you so much, not always knowing what to do.
And even though you are far away
Through our child, my love, I still see you.

- Anonymous

WIDOWS AND WIDOWERS have lost those around whom their worlds usually revolve. The basic routine and familiarity of life is snatched away.

Sally's husband died in his early seventies after a three-year battle with cancer. Norm was under hospice care for many months prior to his expected death, yet no amount of preparation had readied Sally for the loss. Even though Norm's suffering was over, Sally's loneliness and pain was just beginning.

The emotional upheaval only made the task of planning a funeral and applying for life insurance and survivor benefits more arduous. Who would manage the household finances? Who could she find to make minor household repairs since her handy-man husband was no longer with her? Would she need a part-time job to make ends meet? Should she sell his vast collection of tools in his workshop or his pick-up truck? What about his clothes, his electric razor, his collection of cowboy boots?

The death of a spouse is rated as one of the most distressing events in life – an event that one of the spouses must eventually face. Such a drastic life-altering occurrence not only brings the pain of grief, but also envelopes one in an overwhelming time of decision making. Such choices can seem almost impossible to make.

After a few months, Sally decided Norm's personal items were too much of a reminder of his death and began giving away many of them. Her family had first choice on those possessions such as his workshop tools and his old truck. She donated most of his clothing to a local charity. It was not that Sally was trying to for-get about Norm. Rather, the constant reminders seemed to only reinforce her sense of loss. Forgetting Norm was impossible and not what she wanted to do. She did find some relief and even gratification in giving others his possessions which she did not need. She saw how much her children appreciated the mementos of their father.

Sally's depression began to improve after about a year, and the intense yearning after about two years. Immersing herself in her gardening in the summer and in sewing in the winter proved ther-apeutic. Supportive neighbors and friends regularly called on her. One of her grand-daughters resided nearby, which gave her many opportunities to spend time with her and her great-grandchildren. After two years, by admitting she had to alter her definition of normal in order to adjust, Sally found life about as normal as she expected it to be without Norm by her side.

Debbie, on the other hand, lost her husband early in their marriage. She and her two young daughters were left without a spouse and father. She tells her story of heartache and healing in the following story:

At the age of 35, I found myself a widow with two nine-year-old daughters to now raise-alone.

How could this have happened? Surely when I repeated the words, "...til death do us part...." they were not supposed to mean after only fifteen years of marriage. Yet the reality of my situation was indeed that death, in the form of malignant melanoma, had parted us. In experiencing the gamut of emotions that follow the loss of a loved one, I think I have encountered a few lessons which I hope will help someone with the tragic loss of a loved one.

Initially, try to avoid major decisions. Even minor decisions which can be put off are best left undone for a time. Rely on the support and assistance of loved ones and friends who offer help. Accept the truth that your decision making skills are not at the best functional level during this time and defer making major choices for a time. You have experienced a life altering change which produces stress of its own. Postpone decisions which may result in additional stress until you realize you are ready to make good choices again. You will now make decisions on your own instead of consulting with a life partner, so give yourself time to adjust to this new role.

Immediately following my husband's death, I believed there would be a time line which I could follow and know that after a certain period of time, the sense of loss would be lessened. In this, I was mistaken. Grief knows no time frame and will be an adjustment that you will eventually make for yourself. I have come to understand that even after a decade, there is seldom a day I do not think of my husband. It is no longer with the mind numbing grief, but thoughts of him are still frequent. The difference is that the overwhelming sadness does not accompany those thoughts now.

You will find that many people are uncomfortable talking about your lost loved one. I have found it beneficial to have a few people who understand your need to continue to talk about this person. You do not want to make your loved one the focus of every conversation, but you will find comfort in having a few people you can speak openly with concerning the person. I explained to a few close friends that because my husband was no longer with us did not mean that he was out of our thoughts. I also asked them not to feel uncomfortable and to please try to understand that there would be a need for us to continue to talk of him.

Fortunately, I have friends who understood that request and responded accordingly. It has been a comfort to continue to talk of him freely with close friends. I also discovered that my daughters drew comfort from meeting people who knew their dad and could tell them things about him. I generally would handle introductions by telling the person that the girls greatly enjoy meeting people who knew their father. That usually sets the person at ease and gives the girls little bits and pieces of information about their father.

I believe the most important thing I could share with anyone is a quite simple but surprising statement. You will be happy again. Make no mistake, you will continue to miss the person whom you have lost, but you will have a full and happy life again. There will be continued moments of grief, but you will find that you will focus more on pleasant memories and happy times. I have enjoyed every moment I have spent with my two children and have made the most of my situation. In a recent conversation with one of my daughters, I was surprised to hear her state that many people would believe the loss of her father would make her life otherwise, but that she believed she was a very happy and fortunate person despite her loss.

Life goes on, and you will continue on as well. You will grow and find yourself whole again. I was surprised to have a co-worker who had been widowed to tell me that I was her inspiration. Although I had tried to speak to her and offer comfort, I had been cautious not to remind her of her situation too frequently. I asked how I could have been an inspiration, and she informed me that when she saw me, she saw a happy person who enjoyed life and knew that meant she could also be happy again. Take every moment you need to grieve and even to pamper yourself on occasion, but continue to enjoy life, the things you love, and those you love.

When a recently widowed young mother relived her tragedy during an office visit, Debbie is the person I soon contacted to call and encourage this struggling lady. She was better able to understand than those of us who had not experienced widowhood. Each time I see Debbie or her daughters, I am encouraged and inspired by their emotional strength and courage.

Another patient, Jennifer, lost her husband to a brain tumor a few months before his fortieth birthday. With a ten year old son, a mortgage, a car payment and a meager life insurance policy, Jennifer was overcome by grief, parental responsibilities and financial obligations which she never anticipated. Her situation was complicated by the death of her elderly mother six months before her husband died. The first eight months of mourning after her husband's death were unbearable as she now grieved for not one but two loved ones. She became reclusive, depressed and developed insomnia. I prescribed a daily antidepressant and an occasional sleeping pill to help her adjust. She soon found her only relief from the painful yearning was the time she was asleep.

Since the only time she could sleep was when she took a sleeping pill, she began taking them during the day as well as at bedtime.

As you may suspect, this interfered with her job, her parental and home duties. While mom was secluded in her bed most of the day and night, her son was grieving in his own cocoon of video games and music. He ignored his homework and almost failed a year of school. The lack of parental guidance resulted in poor nutrition, hygiene and study habits.

Jennifer's abuse of her medications eventually resulted in a single-vehicle traffic accident when she dozed while driving and sustained minor injuries. The accident served as a wake up call from abusing the sleeping pills and Jennifer soon came to my office to discuss the incident. She needed no chiding since she realized the spiral of grief and medication abuse was stealing her life from her and her son.

We mutually agreed upon some changes in her medication that helped with the depression and apathy. There were no more episodes of taking sleeping pills during the day. She and her son met regularly with a counselor, and over the next few months the depression began to clear. Within a few weeks of starting counseling she was able to work full-time and meet her financial obligations. She and her son began walking together every evening as exercise. As she began to function normally, her son's behavior and grades remarkably improved. It took about three years for Jennifer to find her emotional equilibrium, but she finally overcame the depression and insomnia.

Despair and depression are inevitable consorts to grief, but these and other troubling emotions can be managed by allowing others to share the burden, by seeking help when needed and by prompting ourselves to move forward. My Aunt Norma told me years later that after months of grieving, she realized she had a small child that needed to be reared and it was time to move forward with her life and his. Robert Frost commented, "In three words I can sum up everything I've learned about life: it goes on".

CHAPTER SIX:
THE BROKENHEARTED

"When fever and illness came, the practitioner cured with his art.
But with what remedy now, shall my healer mend this broken heart?"

THE TWO PRECEDING lines are a poetic paraphrase of a common complaint heard by physicians. Grief is not limited to those who have lost a loved one, but can occur in many other instances. Suturing a laceration, healing an infection or treating a sprain is a much easier task than treating a broken heart.

The term *broken hearted* is actually a state of grief which is usually associated with a romantic loss. The spurned lover and the betrayed spouse both experience vivid times of painful mourning.

For instance, Katie is a lovely teenager in a military family. When her family was re-stationed from Europe to a facility near our community, she met a dashing young 16-year-old named Kirk, who soon became her heartthrob.

After falling in love, they were intimate several times within the first few weeks of their relationship. Katie was certain she wanted to spend the rest of her life with Kirk, but unbeknown to her, he was not as committed to the relationship as she. Four months after their relationship began, Kirk decided the chemistry between them was not what he wanted. He soon moved on to another romance with one of Katie's friends whom he had been courting while seeing Katie. This other young lady also fell in love with this popular young man.

Katie came to see me (at the insistence of her parents) for symptoms of depression. She had lost weight and no longer enjoyed tennis or track. Her grades dropped significantly and she even failed one of her classes. She would come home from school and go straight to her room where she would cry for what seemed like hours. Neither her parents nor friends could console her. Katie was short-tempered with her mom and dad as well as with her teachers and became very irritable. She withdrew from her friends and lost concern for her appearance. Secretly, she experimented with drugs to ease her mind. This behavior went on for months before her mother insisted she seek medical advice.

Katie knew the source of her depression and it only took a few minutes of conversation with her to learn what precipitated her sorrow. Katie was grieving over a lost relationship. She had a broken heart. We talked about the relationship she shared with Kirk and how much she missed him. Because she was planning on eventually marrying him, it seemed as if Katie had lost a spouse.

Katie was lost in her grief. At a young age, she had given her love and trust to a young man to whom she was deeply committed. More than a year after the break-up, she still thought of Kirk most free minutes of the day. She occasionally saw him at school with her former friend (now Kirk's newest girlfriend) which only served to compound her grief.

Katie lost a relationship - a relationship in which she invested herself emotionally and physically. I would suggest that their intimate physical relationship deepened an emotional and even a spiritual relationship between them that is difficult to scientifically explain - yet Katie could clearly see it. Although she felt she had loved another young man a year earlier before moving back to the states, her intimacy with Kirk formed a bond which she could not seem to break. It was as if the lost relationship was a beautifully woven cloth that has been stained and ripped apart with the ragged edges still showing. Dozens of times a day, Katie thought she was re-living the past. At the slightest reminder of Kirk the pain would resurge. Old movie ticket stubs or photos found in a dresser drawer could easily cause an agonizing flashback

Even though they were not married, Katie feels as if she and Kirk were. She lost something within herself. At her young age, her story is similar to those who lost a spouse to death or divorce. Such losses cause an obvious physical void as well as an unexplainable emotional and spiritual void. They have indeed lost a part of themselves.

In her recovery, Katie inadvertently underwent a sometimes effective treatment called desensitization therapy. She was exposed to the same emotional trigger (seeing Kirk) so many times over the next few months that eventually she adapted (became desensitized to the painful stimuli). Her pain gradually decreased and one morning she woke up and thought to herself that she had been depressed long enough. From that day forward, her sadness improved.

Grief can be so sudden, unexpected and harrowing that some people experience a degree of post-traumatic stress disorder (PTSD). PTSD is often considered as only occurring in those subjected to a life-threatening event. But counselors also find the same painful syndrome developing in persons subjected to instances of emotional disasters.

This problem can affect anyone (including mourners) who experiences a life changing catastrophe. PTSD may occur after betrayal trauma such as when a government turns upon and persecutes the citizens it should protect, when a parent abuses a child or when a highly trusted relationship is betrayed. Much like those who have lost loved ones in an automobile accident or who have experienced a sudden heart attack, emotional upheaval is a traumatic experience which frequently causes psychological disequilibrium and a long period of adjustment.

PTSD includes recurring flashbacks that interfere with one's daily routine and extreme emotional mayhem. In fact, to some degree, many mourners may experience the same. One of the difficulties in dealing with betrayal is that unlike the death of a loved one, it is difficult to find closure. You may still live (and may be trying to rebuild) with the one who caused such pain.

Patty, for instance, is a young lady that has experienced grief due to marital failure. She is an attractive and well educated young woman with three beautiful girls. She married the young man of her dreams only to discover a few years later he had a drug and alcohol problem. After years of Tom's treatment programs, unpaid bills, legal problems, extra-marital affairs and repeated separations, Patty finally gave up on any hope that the marriage would survive and filed for divorce.

At first, Tom was again repentant and pleaded for her to give him one more chance. When she explained that she couldn't take it anymore, he became furious and began drinking again. This led to more episodes of verbal abuse, domestic disturbances and police visits to keep Tom away from Patty and the girls. Prior to the divorce, their home was foreclosed on and their meager savings were wasted. Now Patty and the girls live in a cramped apartment. She works two jobs to support the girls since Tom's child support payments are habitually late.

Even after divorcing, the ill-effects of their failed marriage continue to plague Patty and her daughters. Simply the sight of the man she once loved brings back reminders of the pain inflicted during the twelve difficult years of their marriage. As a single mom, she relies on the limited child support that Tom tries to pay each month. She still must deal with seeing him when the girls visit with their father. On holidays she has to arrange for time when the girls can see Tom.

Some days Tom does not work due to relapses. During those times Patty must cope with his altered mental state when he tries to contact the girls. Police visits are still occasionally required to keep Tom away when he drinks. There are many nights that she hears her girls crying for their dad, and soon thereafter she sobs along with them.

Patty's daughters struggled with the loss of daily contact with a beloved parent. Although their parents attempted to shield them from all the details of the strained marriage and bitter divorce, they witnessed the struggles of their parent's failed relationship. The oldest daughter continues to strive to be the strong supporter and big sister to her siblings, but the second daughter, age nine, withdrew emotionally from her family and friends. She immersed herself in her studies and her grades actually improved as the marriage deteriorated and the divorce ensued. Academics became her haven from the harsh reality of her home life. Patty continues to strive to emotionally connect with her, but since the divorce her daughter seems emotionally anesthetized and withdrawn.

Emotionally disconnecting serves as a protective maneuver for children and adults alike. Much like the initial emotional numbness of grief, this prolonged detachment may lead to a lower level of pain for the one hurting. But as the protective emotional shell persists it may also lead to difficulties later in life in forming close relationships with others.

Even though they have been divorced for several years, Patty feels as if she has made slow progress to recover emotionally. She feels guilty when saying life would have been easier for her and her children if Tom had died. At least she would have some closure and time to heal. With Tom and his addiction still a part of her life, she feels as if each time she heals somewhat, another crisis causes the throbbing to start over again.

Many estranged or divorced couples have similar stories of how the pain of addictions, infidelity, lies, physical and/or verbal abuse have destroyed the most cherished of relationships. Even though there is no funeral to attend, no obituary to announce the mourning, and no wake to hold, their grief and suffering is just as real as if someone had died.

In spite of the hindrances, Patty is finding ways to move forward by occupying herself and her daughters. Although working more hours than she wishes, the time at her jobs helps divert her thoughts from her loss. Any free time she can extract from her day, she spends biking or jogging at a local park with her girls. Patty finds perspiring therapeutic.

Exercise can be both a pastime and potent remedy for many medical conditions as it releases natural brain endorphins into the bloodstream. These endorphins act as natural pain relievers and antidepressants. For a brief time she took an antidepressant, but soon felt she could do without it.

She is slowly becoming able to support her children. She has learned to expect Tom's relapses and in anticipating them, she no longer finds them surprising to the point of causing another emotional crisis. Patty admits that while work has its stressors, it can be a welcome relief when compared to sitting at home with her sorrow and worry.

Patty feels as if she is gun-shy to any new romantic relationships, so she is avoiding any at present, but admits she hopes the day will come when she is comfortable dating again. Joining the Girl Scouts has become a mother-daughter adventure, and although the busyness of work, managing a home and being a single mom can be overpowering, for Patty and her daughters, these activities have helped them cope and move on with life.

CHAPTER SEVEN:
THE GRIEF RESPONSE

I awaken when I should be resting,
Long before the sun arises
And wonder why I feel so uneasy,
Only to be soon reminded.

I reach for my loved one across the bed,
As I did for so many years,
Alas, there I find a cold pillow
That now serves to muffle my tears.

On nights like this I miss you so dearly
And wish this pain could have a cure.
Yet the fond memories you left with me
Help me find the strength to endure.

Why was I not allowed to go with you?
Surely there must be some reason.
So now I wait, and long again
To see you, in God's good season.

-Anonymous

WHILE LIVING THROUGH the aftermath of the death of someone close to us, often it helps to know some of the emotions to expect, as well as a general time frame in which they may come. Even though grief is an all too common event for mankind, each person's bereavement is exquisitely painful.

Approximately two million deaths occur each year in the United States. Considering this statistic and the number of relatives and friends affected by each death, we can estimate that there are close to twenty million new episodes of grief due to death each year in America. Yet no two episodes are exactly the same because our emotional relationships to the deceased are like no other. While grief is all too common, it is still unique to the mourner.

Death is not the only cause of grief. Therefore, the actual number of newly bereaved individuals is, in fact, much higher than the twenty million a year - and this is in the United States alone.

Mourning is a painfully slow event for most of us. Try to not be discouraged when it seems that you are progressing slower than you would expect. Nor should you feel guilty if some aspects of your mourning seem to pass more quickly than "normal". Your grief is yours to bear in your own manner and on your own timetable.

Recognizing your grief as unique will keep you from comparing yourself to others. It will allow you to work through your emotions at your own tempo. In time, the pain will slowly ease and somehow, someway, life will continue. In the meantime, undeniably there will be some very, very difficult days and nights to endure.

We often use the words *grief, mourning* and *bereavement* interchangeably, yet they have somewhat different definitions. **Grief** signifies an intense emotional suffering caused by a loss, disaster or misfortune. We usually use this word when describing the storm of emotions following the death of a loved one. We can also grieve heavily over the loss of a home, a job, a pet or over divorce, infidelity or other romantic disappointment.

Grief can occur as the result of losing one's health as can be seen in chronic or terminal illnesses, or after the loss of an arm or leg due to an amputation. We may grieve after an involuntary move from one city filled with friends and familiar sites to another one filled with strangers and uncertainties. War or natural disasters may precipitate grief. Not all, but some elderly people may grieve when the time comes to give up their independence and, if necessary, live with relatives, move to a nursing home or other assisted care facility.

Bereavement is from the Old English word "berefian". To bereave means to deprive, rob or to leave in a sad or lonely state. The word denotes that the situation has been encountered involuntarily and forced upon us. Bereavement is almost invariably reluctantly endured. The word bereavement is almost exclusively used to designate the period of time after the death of a loved one.

Mourning suggests the display of sorrow with an anxious mindfulness of someone or something we have lost. Mourning may vary according to particular cultures, social norms, or family traditions. In some countries, the death of a loved one would be followed by an uninhibited show of emotion by all family members and friends in both private and public. Professional mourners may be employed to demonstrate the depth of a family's loss. In other cultures, a very somber and quiet mourning period would follow the loss. Both situations would be considered normal for their respective cultures.

Although the definitions of grief, bereavement and mourning are somewhat different, their meanings are usually understood to be very similar. They all encompass the emotions of profound sadness and frequent longing for that which is lost.

When we know that a loved one has a terminal illness, the surviving family members may experience grief even before the death occurs. This is known as anticipatory grief. If a "normal" course of grief lasts approximately two years, then let us suppose one's anticipatory phase lasted eighteen months. In such a situation, the mourning process after the death may only last six months. This may lead friends and family to believe that the grieving process may not have been as difficult since it did not last as long as one may expect. Yet, the total time of grieving was almost as long as the average two year period of grief since the period of mourning had actually started before the death occurred. While two to three years is a commonly cited time frame for grief to resolve (evolve may be a better term), every situation and relationship is different as will be the mourning thereafter.

In 1968, Elisabeth Kübler-Ross presented her often cited theory of an individual's response to a terminal diagnosis as they anticipate death. She initially described five response phases as one faces death - denial, anger, bargaining, depression and acceptance. Sometimes the theory is also used as a framework for a grief model, yet bereavement experts have shown that the mourning process is somewhat different than the response to an illness with a deadly prognosis. Phillip Yancey has noted that Leo Tolstoy may deserve some credit as well for the grief model since he presented a similar view of these stages in *The Death of Ivan Ilych,* although he never actually labeled the phases in his 1860's publication.

While these are generalized phases, they do not always proceed in orderly fashion, and an individual may move back and forth between the different phases. More than one phase may coexist.

These stages do bear some semblance to the phases of grief, but in mourning there is usually little for which to bargain. We have already lost someone or something dear to us that cannot be replaced. While grief certainly involves denial, it may or may not involve anger. While we may be in denial over the death of a dear grandparent who died at the age 110, we are unlikely to be angry for long, if at all. A death at that age would seem to be in the natural order of life and death. It is also certain that patients given terminal diagnoses would grieve during their responses to their illnesses since there is much overlap in the two response models.

The initial grief response to death is often emotional anesthesia. "Surreal" or "numb" are words often used to describe the sensation that follows in the hours, days or even weeks after the tragedy. It is as if we are in an emotional state of shock. This may be our mind's way of softening the emotional blow and allowing for a gradual realization. As the days progress, we slowly perceive more deeply the pain that comes from irretrievably losing someone who is irreplaceable.

For instance, Sally lost her husband, Harold, to metastatic cancer. Even though the diagnosis was made two years prior to his death and she knew for months that the end was near, the death of her husband of 58 years was terribly difficult. She had lost a daughter thirty years earlier and felt that Harold's death was more difficult to bear than the loss of her daughter. Even though the grieving for her child seemed to last longer, Harold's death was even more difficult for her to accept.

"I just can't believe he's gone," was one of the first things she told me after Harold died. She elaborated, "For several days after the funeral it was as if he was still at home or in his workshop or in the garden. And for weeks after he died, at any moment I still expected him to walk in the kitchen door. Sometimes I would even think I was hearing him call my name from down the hall."

Even though Sally knew Harold was going to die, the actual death was still more of a blow than expected. It took about two or three weeks before Sally realized the full weight of her loss. It was then that the emotional anesthesia began to fade.

For Sally and many other mourners, the anesthesia all too soon gives way to the painful reality of grief. A potpourri of emotions will come and go without permission from us. At one moment we may be on solid emotional ground, only minutes later to find ourselves hopelessly lost in a mire of sorrow and tears. We may experience anger, guilt, sadness, depression or relief in varying orders of succession or struggle with them all at once. These emotions seem to come in unannounced waves from minutes to days apart. Grief counselor Ed Ike uses the term, "waves of grief" to describe the recurrent episodes we feel. Each wave may seem as if the mourning process is starting all over again.

The toll of grief goes beyond an emotional cost. Certainly our mental struggles will also affect our physical health. The nervous system chemicals that contribute to our emotional state also affect other parts of our bodies. Fatigue is a common complaint during the emotional and physical toil of grieving. You may find yourself overeating, eating too little or doing both on any given day. Insomnia is common under these circumstances and may take months or years to improve. Anxiety is a frequent component of bereavement and will contribute to irritability and mood swings which will eventually level out.

Grieving people often feel as if they are going insane. This is a common misconception in mourning. Rest assured, your emotional balance will return. But for now, you are bearing a tremendous emotional burden. You will long for normal days and nights, but initially they will be difficult to find.

Try not to be overly discouraged if it takes weeks, months or even a year or two to find a single day that seems normal. Don't plan on completely forgetting your loss - it will never be forgotten. But be assured that you can still experience good days again at some point in the future.

It is a well-described medical phenomenon that existing medical problems can be exacerbated by any type of stress including the profound burden of mourning. It is not unusual for angina, depression, high blood pressure, asthma, skin disorders, migraines, gastrointestinal problems or other conditions to exacerbate during the grieving process. These occurrences are not imagined but are due to chemical changes throughout your body which accompany bereavement.

The region of the brain that senses pain recognizes physical as well as emotional pain. Either type of pain can cause tremendous anguish to a person. Emotional pain is just as real and just as excruciating as physical pain. Some would say even more so.

The emotional pain recognition site in the brain is located near the region that senses and interprets sensations (including pain) from the stomach and other abdominal organs. This explains why we feel an intense aching in our upper abdomen and lower chest when we suffer emotionally. This also accounts for the fact that bad news can elicit nausea to the point of causing one to vomit. Heart attack victims often describe their pain as excruciating and accompanied by a sense of dread. Mourners often note their severe mental pain is accompanied by persistent trepidation.

The mind responds in the pain recognition site by releasing neurochemicals that not only perceive pain but also account for the feelings of rejection, despondency, loneliness and grief. All these undesirable emotions are frequently related to a "sick feeling in our stomach" or an "aching heart". Indeed, the brain actually feels emotional pain as a heart-ache.

Anti-depressants work in the pain recognition site of the brain to increase the level of neurotransmitters such as serotonin and norepinephrine. These compounds are abnormally low in the brains of both a grieving and a depressed person. They are also decreased in the brain of many individuals with chronic pain syndromes.

This explains why persons treated with anti-depressants often experience a decrease not only in emotional, but also in physical pain. Using an anti-depressant in a grieving or depressed person can ease their emotional pain while also improving their mood and outlook.

Not every mourner desires or needs anti-depressants nor should medication be considered a quick and reliable cure for bereavement. But they can be very helpful in such a stressful period.

I discuss the role of pharmaceuticals in more detail in the next chapter.

Don't hesitate to see your physician for advice and help as you go through this difficult time. You may not feel up to attending to your own health, but you must do so in order to allow the emotional wound to heal. The fact that you may need help is not a sign of weakness but rather is a sign of the severe emotional toil with which you are dealing.

Seeking support shows that you recognize the profound stress of grief and that you are proactively doing something to deal with it. Asking for help displays a person's determination to overcome tragedy and to not accept depression as permanent. Even the fact that you are reading this book shows that you are looking for answers, are willing to heal and are being proactive in your recovery.

It is natural and unavoidable for us to think constantly of the one we miss so dearly. We are accustomed to the presence, the conversation, the likes and dislikes, the idiosyncrasies and the imperfections of our loved one. Life is no longer the same without them, and it never will be. However, life can be good again in time.

For example, Mr. and Mrs. Long were patients who came to see me for years and always seemed to be at odds with each other. They were somewhat sarcastic in their comments toward one another and seemed to have lost the romance somewhere along the way. Yet, the fact that when one would pause in speaking the other would invariably complete the sentence, gave the impression that they were emotionally attached at the hip.

After sixty years of marriage, they thought alike, spoke alike and were even beginning to look somewhat alike - more like siblings in appearance than spouses. I listened to them on more than one occasion frankly point out the other's faults over the years. One might say they couldn't live happily together nor live happily apart.

This was very obvious when Mr. Long passed away. Mrs. Long

was as out of place as a meditating monk at the mall. In addition to struggling with the expected grief, she no longer had anyone to complain with or to, no one to argue with and no one to complete her train of thought. They had become comfortable with each other's quirks and sarcasm. She missed the mental sparring with her partner.

It was not that she regretted any of her or his complaining over the years, nor their cutting comments to each other. She missed the emotional encounters to which she was accustomed. In spite of his frequent sarcastic complaints and blatant imperfections, she dearly grieved for Mr. Long.

Grief robs us of an emotional savings account. Keep in mind that you were accustomed to receiving emotional dividends from years of emotional investments in a relationship that you no longer will receive in similar fashion. Hopefully, we have invested in other emotional relationships where we can draw some emotional support, but it will not be the same.

Losing a close relationship is a bitter loss. It may help to remember that our loved one does live on in our memories and in many cases in posterity. My grandfather was able to find some solace in the fact that his deceased son's son lived on to bring him joy in life. So in some ways, you still can benefit emotionally from the relationship. Admittedly, it is a bittersweet dividend.

Even if the relationship was less than perfect, we miss the familiarity and security we had at one time. We cannot help thinking of our loved one, and at times it may seem as if the harder we try to avoid remembering, the more difficult it is to forget. It is much like the insomniac who tries more diligently to fall asleep only to find his efforts keep him awake.

For most of us, forgetting the source of our grief is impossible. If allowed, the mourning process will teach us to live with the memories and constant reminders of all that was lost. And in time, you will gradually be able to enjoy some pleasant memories. At some point you will be able to think not only of your loss, but also of the good times you shared with your loved one. It may take many months or many years before the adjustment is made, but with effort and time, along with the help of family and friends it will eventually occur.

Chapter Eight:
The Phases of Grief

*"You can clutch the past so tightly to your chest that it leaves
your arms too full to embrace the present."*
-Jan Glidewell

*"There are things that we don't want to happen but have to accept,
things we don't want to know but have to learn,
and people we can't live without but have to let go."*
-Unknown

SEVERAL AUTHORS HAVE attempted to classify the stages of grief. As you will see, these stages are described somewhat differently than the phases of accepting a terminal illness, which we discussed earlier. While it is not an exact science, many writers have well described some of the emotional responses we experience with mourning.

In the early 1960's, Dr. John Bowbly and Dr. Colin Parkes were among the first in modern medical literature to publish their proposed stages of grief. These would include shock-numbness, yearning-searching, disorganization-despair, and reorganization. Dr. Kubler-Ross built upon this work in describing the five phases in response to a terminal illness.

J. William Worden, Ph.D., described four "tasks of mourning". They include accepting the loss as real, experiencing the pain of the grief, adjusting to the environment where the deceased is no longer present, withdrawing emotional energy from the former relationship and redirecting that investment of energy into new relationships and activities.

Building a new relationship does not necessarily mean attempting to replace a spouse or to have another child since the one lost can never be replaced. While some widows and widowers eventually remarry, doing so should not be done in attempt to recover the lost relationship. New relationships should be built upon mutual attraction, love and compatibility. Otherwise, the new partner will likely be continually compared to the former one (even in a healthy new relationship, this may sometimes occur).

Activities of interest such as work or hobbies can be therapeutic. Co-workers may wonder why a grieving spouse may return to work so soon after their loss, but an active workplace may be a welcome reprieve from a silent and lonely house. A home loses much of its emotional security when there is no one left with whom to share it.

Elizabeth Harper Neeld, Ph.D., describes her findings of grief in her book *Seven Choices of Grief.* Although the term "choice" may not be the first word that comes to mind in grief, the word "crisis" can be substituted in its place. She describes the first choice as the initial impact (or crisis). This occurs when we first learn of bad news, such as the death of a family member. This is the time of emotional anesthesia or mental reluctance to accept the death as real.

Next comes the second choice/crisis when the emotional anesthesia begins to wear away and the tremendous burden of grief settles upon us. The third choice is a time of recollection of memories and a time of observation. Fourth, comes "the turn", where we adjust to a new life without our loved one. This fourth choice is more of a conscious decision than the prior three crises, as are the last choices. The fifth and sixth choices involve a time of releasing the old emotional bonds and redirecting that energy into new relationships. Finally, choice seven is a time when we can enjoy the good memories of the lost relationship without the mind numbing grief accompanying those thoughts.

Another author, Theresa Rando, Ph.D., observes three general phases of grief. These include Avoidance, Confrontation and Accommodation. She subdivides these phases with her list of the Six "R" Processes of Mourning. Avoidance is a time of mental anesthesia followed by denial. While denial may be initially good for us in order that certain arrangements be made, it should not go on for such a long time that the next phase of mourning cannot be reached within a few weeks or so. This is the time for *recognizing* the loss.

Confrontation is the next painful process of realizing what has happened and the severity of our loss. It is a time of emotional searching for the return of something irretrievable. This is when an intense separation anxiety comes upon us. Periods of denial may still intermittently occur for months or years to come. This phase usually brings a wide array of intense emotions from profound sadness to bitter anger to frustrating confusion. This is when we *react* to the loss, *recollect* and re-experience the lost relationship, and *relinquish* old attachments and bonds with the loved one.

The accommodation phase occurs when the acute grief evolves into the acceptance of the tragedy and we then allow ourselves to move forward. As we do, we accept the enduring memories while we develop new relationships. This is the time when we *readjust* and *reinvest*. Rando defines accommodation to mean that the mourner can integrate the past with the present and the new person that now exists. Rando says, "The mourner will never forget, but she will not always be acutely bereaved. Accommodating the loss will leave a psychic scar, similar to a scar that remains after a physical injury. This scar does not necessarily interfere with the mourner's overall functioning, but on certain days and under particular conditions it may ache or throb. It will remind the mourner of what she has been through and that she must tend to her feelings until the pain passes".

Studies by Dr. Selby Jacobs were published in the early 1990's. His research pointed to four generalized sequential stages. These stages include numbness-disbelief, separation distress (yearning-anger-anxiety), depression-mourning, and recovery.

Dr. Paul Maciejewski presented a paper to the *Journal of the American Medical Association* in 2007 that questioned about 300 individuals concerning their response to grief. In comparison to prior studies, this research indicated that while all the stages described by Dr. Jacobs are common, acceptance often occurs earlier than expected and grows during the time of grieving after a natural death. Intense yearning for the deceased was also one of the most common experiences noted and subsided somewhat over time. Depression was reported as the next most frequently experienced emotion. All the emotions seemed to peak and then improve after about two years.

When faced with grief, most of us will experience all of these emotions at some point. There will be days when we feel them all at once. Even after we are sure we have healed, some moments will still find us engulfed in brief periods that remind us of our loss.

As can be seen from the varied research results, reducing grief to a predictable formula is improbable since a blueprint of grieving is slightly different for each of us. While life with grief seems disordered and unfocused, there will eventually emerge a pattern of gradual healing and a return to normality.

CHAPTER NINE:
THE DEPRESSION OF GRIEF

Alone I sit for my dinner again.
Months after we laid you to rest,
And family and friends have tried to console
By saying I'm doing my best.

But if they could know how lonely I am,
Dining for one, rather than two.
Tears for my drink, grief for dessert,
And an entrée of missing you.

I miss reaching for your hand to say grace,
Dining, laughing, being content.
What I would give for one more quiet dinner
With you to savor your presence.

Life cannot always be as I so choose,
With grief, I must learn it anew.
I accept that you are not here tonight,
But not life less memories of you.

The days are easier, I must admit,
But the healing - it takes so long.
You told me I was strong, so heal I must,
With thoughts of you leading me on.

But those very same thoughts make it so hard,
They remind me of things now gone.
Bittersweet reminders, of you, of us,
Strengthen me as my love lives on.

So what will I say for my grace tonight?
Grateful I am, ev'n in sorrow,
I give thanks for good days gone by, for love,
And for the hope of tomorrow.

-R.C. Choala

FOR MOST OF US, the death of a close friend or family member results in a type of depression. Depression often results from a profound sense of unredeemable loss accompanied by perceived hopelessness. Your mood will undoubtedly be a depressed mood on many days for months and months to come. In fact, your state of mind is described in medical text books as a Bereavement Reaction or a Reactive Depression (but for most of us, the simple term depression seems appropriate and is commonly used). It very closely resembles clinical depression which is also known as a Major Depressive Disorder. Let's look at each of these clinical conditions.

With a Major Depressive Disorder, the reason for a person's depression is not usually readily apparent or is even nonexistent. As opposed to grieving individuals, people with a Major Depressive episode are usually more reluctant to accept the help and support of those around them.

Lack of both energy and enthusiasm for life exists for months or even years on end. Major Depression seems to run in families, although it may not affect all generations to the same extent. Thoughts of suicide frequently occur in Major Depression as well as in grief, but grieving individuals will usually recognize these thoughts as irrational and will be able to control them. If not, you should speak to either your doctor or a grief counselor for advice and support.

Grieving individuals can easily identify the cause of their depressed mood. It is because of some physical and/or emotional loss in their lives, and they usually will try to accept support from family and friends. Bereaved persons often experience more of an agitated, anxious or even an angry type of depressed mood than those going through a Major Depression.

After a few weeks or months the mood will gradually begin to improve, but there will still be days when it seems as if the grief is starting all over again. This recurrent cycle of grief may last for a few months or even years, but there should be a gradual overall improvement in well being as time progresses. Keep in mind that the healing which occurs during mourning may take *excruciating effort.*

The following excerpt comes from *The Diagnostic and Statistical Manual of the American Psychiatric Association* and describes bereavement.

> The term bereavement can be used when the focus of clinical attention is a reaction to the death of a loved one. As part of their reaction to the loss, some grieving individuals present with symptoms characteristic of a Major Depressive Episode (e.g., feelings of sadness and associated symptoms such as insomnia, poor appetite, and weight loss).
>
> The bereaved individual typically regards the depressed mood as "normal", although the person may seek

professional help for relief of associated symptoms such as insomnia or anorexia. The duration and expression of "normal" bereavement vary considerably among different cultural groups. The diagnosis of Major Depressive Disorder is generally not given unless the symptoms are still present two months after the loss.

However, the presence of certain symptoms that are not characteristic of a "normal" grief reaction may be helpful in differentiating bereavement from a Major Depressive Episode. These include 1) guilt about things other than actions taken or not taken by the survivor at the time of death; 2) thoughts of death other than the survivor feeling that he or she would be better off dead or should have died with the deceased person; 3) morbid preoccupation with worthlessness; 4) marked psychomotor retardation; 5) prolonged and marked functional impairment; and 6)hallucinatory experiences other than thinking that he or she hears the voice of, or transiently sees the image of, the deceased person.

Psychomotor retardation refers to the slowing of thought and physical reaction time. This may result in a hesitation to respond in conversation or struggling with simple calculations such as following recipes. It may also cause problems with activities such as driving. Functional impairment is a logical consequence of the psychomotor issue and occurs when one has difficulty fulfilling their job or social obligations due to the bereavement.

Please note that most bereavement counselors would agree with all of the above criteria *except* the time frame of two months. Actually, most mourning will last upwards of two years or more. In complicated grieving bereavement may last for many decades or even a lifetime.

To answer a frequent question, "Am I depressed?" most likely you are and understandably so. The depression of grief is not abnormal, though. It is to be expected for some time to come and that period of time will vary from person to person. Depression is a natural part of grief.

Remember that no one else has exactly the same memories to recall, has lost the exact same relationship nor has to bear the exact same grief as you. While the bereavement of others may be similar and their pain just as intolerable as yours, the grief you are living with is as unique as your fingerprint.

Your healing will likely be a little different from others, yet the way you deal with this struggle may in the future help someone else deal with their grief. Undoubtedly, you will at some point in your life have the opportunity to share your story or just your support with someone who will need it. You may find that simply being a help to others will emotionally brighten your own day and lighten your own burden.

There may come a time when you alone can truly understand what another grieving individual is experiencing. Providing support and true empathy for someone who struggles with grief will help you find some good from your grief in the midst of your dark days. Investing concern in the life of another will enrich your own life.

In my early years of practicing medicine, I was reluctant to ask an individual such as Debbie to share their struggles with another person who was going through a similar situation. As a young widow, Debbie was the best informal counselor I could recommend to a recently widowed young mother. I have been pleasantly surprised to see the good that comes to both individuals. The encourager finds value in sharing their past hardship and the mourner finds solace in knowing someone else has encountered and survived a similar disaster.

The pain, yearning and depression associated with grief will invariably interfere with your daily routine for at least a few weeks after the death. Within a few months following, hopefully you will find the energy and effort necessary to go about your daily routine.

Don't be surprised if you need a few moments each day for many, many months to be alone and even to weep. This is a natural process that will help you heal. Not all individuals will feel the need to cry, but most of us will find that we feel relieved afterward. It is as if the tears wash some of the pain away - at least for a time. This is your mind's way of emotionally cleansing and refreshing itself. You may find moments in your day when you are unable to express your emotions freely, but whenever you can be alone (or accompanied by someone with whom you are comfortable), allowing yourself to weep will help release some of the emotional burden. Don't overly suppress or avoid this healing process since it will help in bringing restoration to your emotions. Tears are not a sign of weakness. At the appropriate time, they can be a means to renewing one's strength.

If in a few months you find you just cannot bring yourself to go about your daily routine or return to work, consider meeting with a bereavement counselor who is trained to help you work through this experience. Do not consider yourself a failure if you need some help in working through this exquisitely painful process. Grief is one of the most difficult times an individual can experience.

Bereavement counselors are prepared to guide you through the grieving process. They are available for individual or family counseling either for only one or two sessions or for regular follow up visits for many months. And again, consider speaking with your physician about your physical symptoms. Medication will not be a quick nor easy solution for you, but it very well may help tide you over while you work through the burdensome task of grieving.

Antidepressants can be used on a temporary basis (a few months to a few years) to help with the anxiety and depression that frequently occur with bereavement. These medications often will also aid in treating insomnia. Inadequate rest may hinder your healing. Some types of antidepressants will also help with the lack of concentration that may accompany grief. These medications are often the best choice for a grieving individual. Some patients will find them helpful for a few weeks, while others find them useful for many months.

You and your physician should decide together when and if it is time to start a medication and also at a follow-up visit discuss when it would be appropriate to discontinue it. A course of at least six to nine months would be helpful for most individuals. If needed, a treatment time of one to two years, or even longer, would not be unreasonable.

Although some grief counselors have suggested that medication may postpone the inevitable pain of grief, I tend to agree with other researchers who suggest that medication can be very helpful in mourning. Just as pain medicine gives relief to a healing burn injury, antidepressants can make grief somewhat more bearable. While they can help ease some of the pain of mourning, they are not a cure. The healing of grief comes only through experiencing it, accepting it and with the passage of time.

Complicated grieving is the subject of many books and a comprehensive review of the topic is beyond the scope of this publication. However, we can review some of the symptoms you may be encounter.

Complicated grief is a term used to describe grief that most authorities would consider outside the range of normal for the majority of the population undergoing the same emotional stress. As you may suspect, there is varying opinion among psychologists and physicians as to what is considered normal versus complicated grief.

Most of us would agree that young parents who experience the tragic death of a child would mourn for years to come. Their grief would not be considered abnormal. Yet if an adult child experienced the death of their elderly chronically ill father, their mourning would not be expected to last as long as the young parents.

This does not intend to underestimate the impact of the death of an elderly parent, but is intended to point out that an untimely, tragic death would expectantly result in a very long mourning period thereafter. An untimely death is also more likely to result in complicated grieving, which does not necessarily mean an extended period - although it can.

Complicated grieving more often means a *persistent* denial of the death or of the consequences of the death. It can involve grief that does not seem to be improving in the least after many months of mourning. Complicated grieving frequently is the underlying problem when one turns to alcohol or illicit drugs as a coping mechanism. Unresolved anger and hostility may prolong the grieving period and cause problems with family dynamics.

Chronic medical complaints in a mourner which cannot be elucidated via a history and physical exam by a physician are often due to complicated grieving. Of course, there are many other conditions such as anxiety, post-traumatic stress disorder and past physical abuse which may cause similar complaints. Keep in mind that while medical problems can indeed be caused or exacerbated by the stress of bereavement, these problems should improve with the progression and healing that comes with normal bereavement.

It appears that a certain amount of grief is required for certain events in life. Even though we may postpone it, at some point it must be acknowledged and dealt with for us to go on to healing. This does not invalidate the use of medication when needed and is not to be confused with grief flashbacks (which we will discuss later).

Grief that does not seem to improve after many months or years can also be considered complicated grief. Even though some types of mourning, such as after the death of a child, may go on for years or decades, there should be some overall improvement in an individual's coping mechanisms. While there may, and likely will be, times of recurrent pain and mourning for years to come, one should be able to at some point allow the good memories to outnumber the painful ones.

Life will go on whether we want it to or not, so we must force ourselves to go on living and to emotionally contribute to those around us in our sphere of influence. Most tragedies in life are unfair and seemingly unbearable. It is in these most difficult of times that we need the support of our family, our faith, our friends and often professional help from our minister, a grief counselor and our doctor. Complicated grieving is certainly one of those times.

Psychologist Ester Shapiro points out that "when assessing the grief experience of any individual or family, we must always keep in mind the extreme upheaval the bereaved is forced to undergo when coping with the loss of a family member. Even the most prolonged and severe grief reactions represent an individual's best efforts to cope with the extraordinary pressures of death and grief".

CHAPTER TEN:
CHOOSE HEALING

How long has it been - two, maybe three years since I cried each and every day?
It was useless to hold back the tears that would not stop. I knew I could
not see you, but I could not stop the intense longing.

Now something strange these past few days - no tears. In fact, no need for them.
Yes, still some pangs, but it doesn't hurt as deeply today. And the thought of
you even prompts an occasional smile and faint reminders of
happiness long subdued.

Could it be a ray of healing has arrived as sunlight reappearing,
after a long dreary winter?

-Ron Casey

HEALING FROM LOSS and through grief seems to take one of two time frames: slow or slower. It is never quick. But as we have discussed, it should gradually improve as time goes on. Time slowly places the painful event farther away from us and lets us develop new, more pleasant emotional thoughts to compete with the painful ones. This healing comes as we accept the past and live today. Often healing allows new relationships to form.

Occasionally the healing process also takes working through bitterness, unresolved issues, forgiveness and guilt (whether real or perceived). Not only does this process sound laborious; at times, it can be complicated.

Unfortunately, this chapter holds no magic potion to heal the broken heart. There is no book nor is there any advice that will provide a quick or easy resolution of grief. It is a slow process regardless of the emotional pace we are accustomed to traveling. The bereavement that lasts a few months can seem like an eternity when we are in the grip of grief's depression.

Often mourners describe time as subjectively irrelevant, as if they temporarily lose their ability to judge the passage of time. You may feel lost in a fog with no true sense of direction in many different areas of your life. Balancing your checkbook may seem like a calculus course. Household chores may feel like forced labor. Strolling around the neighborhood can remind you of a marathon. Well-intentioned friends and family will at times seem clueless as to the emotional upheaval through which you are working. In fairness to them, remember that others cannot understand completely unless they have been through a similar situation.

Try as you may, your emotions may be totally under control at one moment then absolutely unmanageable the next. In addition to depression, you may struggle with guilt, regrets, anger and many other troubling emotions for quite some time. Allowing these and other disconcerting emotions to run their course is part of the process. Experiencing these feelings may be beyond your control, but how you *respond* to them and to those around you is not.

When you are feeling angry or guilty, try to talk it out with someone you respect and trust rather than taking your anger out on them. Tell someone you are angry, but try not to be angry at the person who is listening and trying to comfort you. Often simply expressing in words the anger we are experiencing will help to soothe the anger by acknowledging it. Try to avoid saying words in haste that you may regret at some point in the future.

Perhaps it would be better to write about your emotions. Journaling provides a private outlet to vent erupting emotions. It also allows us to chronicle our progress.

As mentioned before, a large step in walking the path of grief is tolerating the pain and loneliness with which you are living. As we accept the pain as inevitable, we learn to live with it. Even though we can tell ourselves that we must accept the pain, it takes a while for our hearts to accept the situation. Do not be discouraged, for in time your heart and emotions will realize the inevitable fact that you will have to accept this loss.

Emotions can be very persuasive forces in our lives and often compete with our wills. Emotions may be perceived as good, bad or neutral – but they are simply emotions that must be recognized as such. While enjoying the good ones is effortless, tolerating the others is onerous. Emotions may change as quickly as the weather. They seem to have a mind of their own at times, but with enough effort at healing, we can eventually expect them to fall in line with our wills.

While having a reputation for healing, time in and of itself does not completely heal us. Granted, it is in great part the passage of time that allows the healing process to occur. As we noted, the burden becomes less painful as time takes us farther from the painful episode in our life. Our emotional memories fade somewhat as time goes on. But it will also take a conscientious effort on your part to complete the healing.

So as time passes, the grief flashbacks are not as intense on most days as they were soon after the death occurred. Yet there still will be days even years from now when a certain song, fragrance, holiday, anniversary, or a photograph will bring back the pangs of grief. These are also known as *Subsequent Temporary Upsurges of Grief (STUG)* reactions or waves of grief (grief flashbacks) we mentioned earlier.

Try as you may, you will not be able to completely avoid these unpleasant episodes. Fortunately, they should decrease in intensity and frequency as time passes. Don't be surprised if they never completely disappear. But when they do occur, remember that they are a normal reaction. The flashback will pass in a few hours or even in a few minutes or seconds. The further we go in time from the death of our loved one, the shorter the episodes should persist.

How does one ever forget the trauma of death? In reality, we never completely do. There will always be reminders of our loss. A widow cannot help profoundly missing her husband's presence at their daughter's wedding or the birth of a grandchild. A widower cannot avoid remembering his wife as he sits alone at their son's college graduation - not after all the years of high school activities, football games on Friday night, all the classmates being at the house for pool parties and other fond memories. And now, when their son finally graduates from the university, she is not there to share the pride he feels.

One may never completely get over the loss of a life partner after decades of marriage. A widow may never feel complete again after such a profound event. Some widows and widowers who have remarried and are happy with their new partners have mentioned that at times they still mourn over the loss of their first spouse. A new marriage can be healthy and happy, but it is not a cure-all for bereavement.

Dianne reluctantly admitted that she was struggling with bouts of periodic depression four years after her first husband died. One year ago she remarried and felt very blessed and was grateful for her new marriage to Frank. She and Frank became very involved in their community and church, traveled together several times a year and both described their new marriage as happy and healthy.

Yet unknown to Dianne, Frank was having similar emotions after becoming a widower two years prior. When they eventually admitted to each other their occasional longings for the friendships they had lost through the death of a spouse, they found each other a source of understanding. They resisted the temptation to overtly and critically compare each other to their former spouses and found that as their grief took its normal course of healing they began to more fully enjoy their new lives together. Missing the lost spouse does not imply that the new marriage cannot be a wonderful and appropriate relationship, rather it validates the fact that the first marriage was an important relationship that neither new partner should expect to be forgotten.

One aspect of their new marriage that not all older newlyweds enjoy is the support of their adult children. While no one can replace a mother or father, realizing the irreplaceability of their surviving parent's loss and graciously attempting to accept the parent's new spouse helps avoid the potential guilt some widowed persons may experience upon finding a new love in life.

Young children who lose a parent are astutely aware of their absence at church, at extracurricular events and most of all - at home. How do any of us tolerate the void? It is a monumental task, but one that must be done in order to go on with life.

Again, tolerance must be developed in order to heal. It is not a pleasant aspect and there is no easy or simple way to tolerate grief. Although the initial (acute) phase eventually resolves, remember that the long term (chronic) effects of grief may recur from time to time for years to come. They may never go away completely. Yet even the long term effects of bereavement can eventually become more tolerable. It is never pleasant and never easy, but tolerant it can become.

As C.S. Lewis wrote, "It doesn't really matter whether you grip the arms of the dentist's chair or let your hands lie in your lap.

The drill drills on." This is not to say that you cannot do anything to make the pain more bearable. Lewis simply states the fact that the pain will occur whether we want it to or not.

Unresolved issues in life and death are difficult to work through. Regrets are common and most of us will have at least a few when facing grief. How does one go about the seemingly impossible task of asking a deceased spouse or parent forgiveness for things said or those left unsaid? How do we work through the regret of things we should or should not have done? How can we let go of the bitterness that develops with unresolved resentment?

We have all been guilty of saying or doing things we regret and which cannot be retracted or undone. When spouses say harsh words to one another and shortly thereafter one of them is tragically killed in a car accident, there is always the guilt and regret that the surviving spouse is left to resolve. Sometimes it is helpful in this situation to talk it out with the deceased spouse's parents, siblings or with the couple's own children if they are mature enough to listen and comprehend the situation.

Even though we may be the only one to read it, a letter written to the spouse who died will sometimes help toward making amends. Frequently, we have to simply accept the fact that we said or did things that were wrong, and we must not only ask forgiveness of God and man, but also of ourselves.

We may also need to forgive any unresolved offenses of the one who has died. We should do this for our own sake as well, since resentment and bitterness often translate into anxiety and other health problems. Forgiveness toward others and ourselves may not happen at the moment we decide to forgive, as often forgiveness is as much of a process as it is a choice.

It usually takes a decision to forgive followed by the actions that show we are actually doing so before it happens. The emotional relief of forgiveness will come at some point in the future. The greater the offense, the longer it takes to complete the forgiveness and the more emotional work it requires.

Forgiveness in and of itself is not an emotion. Forgiveness is a conscious ongoing commitment to relieve our offender of the emotional or tangible debt they owe (as much as is possible). Forgiveness must sometimes occur without reconciliation of a relationship, such as when a crime or horrendous act has been committed against us or a loved one.

Even when justice is needed (through the legal system) personal forgiveness can be offered. However, this does not relieve the offender of punishment for crimes. We may offer our forgiveness to a drunken driver who is responsible for the death of our child, or to a rapist or child abuser - but we cannot pardon the crime. It is beyond our personal jurisdiction.

Restitution is often an integral part of forgiveness, but when an offender has died, restitution may not be possible. Forgiveness does not remove all consequences of offenses, but rather allows us emotional resolution toward others. It is a promise that often takes time to completely fulfill.

Healing from tragedy will come sooner when the griever makes a conscious effort to heal. This is a task that will take considerable toil. Consider telling yourself, "I will overcome this one day," or "I can survive this difficult time". You may not feel you can really do these things on the difficult days, but forcing yourself to think positive thoughts about your ability to heal and to go on with life will help you in your response to the death of your loved one.

There will be many days when you feel as if you cannot be positive about anything or anyone. This feeling is normal. But keep telling yourself that choosing to heal is a part of the healing process. If you are having difficult days many years after the death, others may feel you are holding on to your grief too long. Consider that this may indeed be the case. If mourning brings extra attention and care into your life which you would not receive otherwise, then you may find it difficult to let go of your grief.

More often than not though, the hurt simply persists intermittently for many months or years whether secondary gain is an issue or not. Consider allowing a trusted friend, relative or counselor to evaluate you on this possibility. At some point, ask that person to provide feedback on your progress.

Don't give up on yourself. Choose healing and choose it on a daily basis. When you have a difficult day, start over the next and choose healing on that new day. Choose good thoughts, even when it is difficult to do so. When grief first comes upon us, it is truly an undertaking to control our thoughts. For quite some time it will be impossible to think of anything else but your loss.

When you awake in the middle of the night, you may have a sickening feeling deep inside. Almost instantaneously you will recall the event which caused this sensation. You may dream of crying, only to awaken to find your pillow damp with tears. It is not an object or person that has to remind you of the loss. Your subconscious mourns as a part of you and will not soon allow you to forget your grief. This is normal and unavoidable.

Rest assured there will come a time when your mind has grieved enough that it will begin to let go of the pain. How long will it take? Small losses in life may take only a few moments to overcome, while major losses may take years before the pain begins to ease. How long the persistent emotional cloud will remain is unpredictable. The greater the loss, the greater amount of time required for recovery. Persons with very good memories may paradoxically find their mental acuity a hindrance during mourning as it may take longer for their painful memories to fade.

And much like the overall grieving process, the time will vary from one individual to another. While we may not be able to completely *control* all our thoughts (much less our emotions) yet as humans, we possess a great deal of ability to *influence* our own thought processes.

This may be next to impossible for weeks or months after our loss, but with much effort it can be done. And rest assured, there will come a time in your journey of grief when the intruding reminders of your pain can be lessened by choosing to think on more pleasant subjects. Note that the key word is "lessened", and not "alleviated". Do not be discouraged if this lessening takes quite some time to accomplish.

When that time comes, you will not awaken every morning with the recurrent emotions of dread and of loss. You will not have to live under the shadow of the cloud of grief indefinitely. You will not teeter on the brink of tears forever. That time will not appear suddenly, but at some point it will come. Yes, there will still be days when the pain will recur during grief flashbacks, but you will not have to live with the dreadful pain on a daily basis.

The acute anxiety and depression of grief occur without much, if any, thought, but as time passes these emotions will eventually be in response to our memories (our thoughts) of our loss. As we eventually regain control of our thought processes, we are able to focus on more positive memories and on other relationships.

As we encourage ourselves – at times even force ourselves – to think on more pleasant subjects our emotions respond in a positive way to positive thoughts. Depressed thoughts lead to depressed emotions. Pleasant thoughts lead to pleasant emotions. In over-simplified terms, this represents cognitive behavior therapy (CBT). Many therapists offer guidance in CBT which may also be used with a short course of antidepressants. CBT represents more than positive thinking. It involves intentional changes in one's thought processes. This takes time, practice, effort and often a counselor's guidance, but at some point you will notice your ability to affect your mood will improve.

Chapter Eleven: Can Any Good Ever Come From This?

"When we honestly ask ourselves which person in our lives means the most to us, we often find that it is those who, instead of giving much advice, solutions, or cures, have chosen rather to share our pain and touch our wounds with a gentle and tender hand. The friend who can be silent with us in a moment of despair or confusion, who can stay with us in an hour of grief and bereavement, who can tolerate not knowing, not curing, not healing and face with us the reality of our powerlessness, that is a friend who cares."
-Henri Nouwen

WHEN WE FIRST experience grief, it is difficult to see how any good can ever come from such a horrendous event in our lives. In fact, for quite some time it may not be worth the emotional effort to look for such an outcome. Some things in life are beyond our understanding and no amount of logic can give them reason. The dividends of grief may take years to compound.

While there is certainly no harm in asking ourselves, our family, our minister or even God, "Why?" many times in life no answer satisfactorily avails itself. For many of us, life's disasters never make sense. But there can be moments where we find a better understanding of our places in life and of the events that shape our lives.

Even though reasons for life's tragedies are rare to find, looking for them is not wrong for us to do. But there may come a time to postpone or even to stop asking questions and focus more on accepting what has happened. Knowing that we cannot change the past is one thing, but accepting that fact into our thought patterns and into our heart will take some time, perhaps years, to accomplish.

At first, there may not be much point in trying to find any good in our grief. Familiar quotes, words of encouragement, favorite poems or passages of scripture that we hold dear may provide little if any support – at least for a time. While grieving, the last thing a mourner wants to hear is that "it must be for the best" or "there must be a reason for this". Even though we may believe that "all things work for good", actually feeling that this is true in such a desperate time is difficult for us. How can a droplet of good come from an avalanche of grief after the death of a child, of a young mother, of a youth killed in war or by a drunk driver? It may be impossible to see at first and perhaps for decades to come. In some situations, we will never see it.

All of us have endured some type of difficult experience in our lives. Yet when we respond to it appropriately, there is personal growth and strength to be gained, even if only through the pain of the event. That does not mean that death, or any other tragedy, in and of itself was a good or right thing. It simply means that even in tragedy, we can force ourselves to go on, to rise above the trauma and to find an area in our lives where we can grow stronger and learn more about human suffering. As we mature in this area of our lives, we eventually are capable of sharing our experience with others and guiding them through their grief and bereavement.

Some of the most effective organizations in the world have developed out of deep despair. Mothers Against Drunk Driving (MADD) developed in 1980 and was founded by a group of ladies enraged by the devastation caused by drunk drivers. Laura Lamb became a quadriplegic at age five months after she and her mom, Cindi, were struck by a repeat offender who was again driving while intoxicated. Several months later, Candice Lightner's 13 year old daughter Cari was killed by a drunk driver. These two moms along with other ladies who were grief stricken by tragedies joined forces to form MADD.

This organization now has chapters worldwide and has contributed greatly to victim's assistance and support programs, alcohol education initiatives and numerous federal and state anti-drunk driving laws which have been enacted by the organization's efforts. The household term "designated driver" was made popular by MADD's public awareness program. While drunk driving is still a huge problem, the efforts of MADD have undoubtedly saved the lives of countless victims and spared many families from untold grief.

World Vision is one of the largest relief organizations in the world. It was founded in 1950 by Dr. Bob Pierce in an effort to bring aid to the thousands of Korean War orphans whom he had witnessed losing their families in the conflict. The initial efforts of World Vision were the catalysts for a world-wide organization that now extends to almost 100 countries around the world. Their focus continues to be feeding and caring for children, but also encompasses bringing care to entire communities.

Alcoholics Anonymous began in the 1930's when a stockbroker and physician met and discussed the hopelessness each of them was experiencing due to alcohol dependence. They, along with other alcoholics, began meeting in a support group to encourage each other and to provide accountability for the group members. In 1939 the basic textbook of the organization was published entitled *Alcoholics Anonymous*. This book contained the core ideas of AA based upon the twelve steps of recovery used by thousands around the world to aid in their own struggles with alcoholism.

The Red Cross organizational ideas were born in 1859. It was then that a young Swiss man, Henry Dunant, witnessed a horrific bloody battle in Italy. The armies of Austria and the Franco-Sardinian alliance had clashed in a fight that left 40,000 men dead or dying on the battlefield. It was Dunant that organized the locals to tend to the wounded as best they could. Upon his return to Switzerland, he led the effort to create a national relief society to assist the war wounded. In October 1863, the International Red Cross Movement was created in Geneva. Its purpose was to provide nonpartisan care to the wounded and sick in wartime. The red cross emblem was adopted as a symbol of neutrality to be used by national relief organizations. Today, there are Red Cross organizations in 175 countries in the world providing disaster relief in times of war as well as in times of peace.

Could there have been a better way for these organizations to have come into being and still have been as effective? A way where no tragedy was the catalyst? Perhaps so. Nevertheless, they didn't happen that way. Some good was salvaged from the emotional wreck. Good crops were grown in life's compost pile.

These organizations didn't develop overnight, or in just a few months. And likely neither will you be able to find much resulting good for quite some time. It will take effort to look for it. So you must strain your emotional eyes to find ways to recycle the waste of life's misfortunes and heartaches. How can you grow from this? How can you help others through this? How can you take a tragedy and make a tool? You can do it with your persistence, your patience, and with help from your family, your friends and your faith.

Was God your strength before your tragedy? Then God still can and will be. God may seem silent or indifferent. Your prayers and meditations may seem fruitless. You may be tempted to doubt and even abandon your faith. In much the same fashion as our hearing may be damaged after a thunderous explosion, our spiritual senses may be numbed after an emotional disaster. This is a normal reaction. But now is the time to depend upon your faith and family – not a time to falter.

It may be a time to examine and fine-tune your beliefs, but not a time to abandon all faith. Rather than lowering your standards, try to raise them to higher levels. Aspire to the higher principles in life. It will take time for your wounded emotions and spirit to be able to find strength and comfort again, but you will. Was your family a great source of help and encouragement in the past? Allow them to be so again, but remember that they and others may need your guidance in trying to comfort you.

Often people are reluctant to bring up the subject of a loss, fearing that they will only serve to remind you of it. Yet, you will almost constantly think of your loss for many months or years to come. You may be the one who needs to bring up the fact that a certain date is your anniversary or the death date of your loved one.

Maybe you could invite family or friends for dinner to remember an anniversary or some other special date. They would feel much more comfortable if you initiated the invitation. Take care not to overburden your guests with a sense of mourning, but attempt to make such a time an occasion of thankful remembrance – even if some tears are mingled with the remembering.

Times such as these do not have to be a celebration per se, but can simply be a time to reflect, to remember and to honor your loved one. At some point, these times may become times of thanksgiving for the love we experienced and memories we still have with us. Gratitude, much like forgiveness, is more of an action and attitude than it is an emotion.

We can be grateful even in the midst of our mourning, although it takes more effort when we are grieving. The first few yearly anniversaries of a death date are always difficult to endure, but as time goes on, the memories can eventually be appreciated and enjoyed once more. Happiness eventually returns and reflections become fond again.

One of the most effective ways to distract our mind from the emotional upheaval of grief is by attempting to be of help to someone else. This may be difficult to do for the first few months. But at some point, try to be an encouragement to others who are in need. Joining a support group may be beneficial. Consider visiting a shut-in relative, a neighbor or a nursing home. Try to be emotionally supportive of those around you at work or home. Become interested in and involved with your friends and family in a way that lets you emotionally invest in their lives in a positive way.

Think of someone who has a need that you can meet, even if it is simply listening to their problems. Investing emotionally in family and friends allows you to withdraw mental energy from a relationship you no longer can invest in and to deposit that energy into new wholesome relationships. This investment helps fill the void in your life. Even though you may not feel like building new friendships or investing more in existing ones, your emotions will eventually follow your will and your actions as you do so.

At the same time, be careful of the types of relationships you build during this time. New romantic relationships should be entered into slowly, and only after an appropriate period of grief. Taking your time in such relationships helps avoid being taken advantage of during such a susceptible phase of life. It also helps avoid regrets later on in the event you realize you made unwise commitments or decisions at a very vulnerable time.

While grief initially may consume every thought and emotion of the day, it will eventually become an emotional backdrop. Investing in others, continuing or acquiring hobbies, and work all have therapeutic value. While a period of rest is appropriate during grief, returning to work may help distract your mind from being continually barraged with reminders of the loss. Work not only provides an income but also brings a sense of purpose and accomplishment when done well.

Every decision we make in life has an effect for our good or our detriment, whether it's eating versus overeating, rest versus sloth or investing versus squandering. The same is true of our relationships. Kind words and actions eventually reap kindness, whereas harsh words and actions do the opposite.

Deciding to heal and to invest in new relationships with friends and family takes much effort and determination. You may not be able to decide today to begin healing and investing emotionally –it may be too soon for such a choice - but at some point you *must* if you plan to heal. The results and rewards will not come immediately, but be assured that they will come in time.

CHAPTER TWELVE:
UNDERSTANDING THE LOSS

It is better to visit the house of the mourning
Than to a house of feasting,
Because that is the end of every man
And the living takes it to heart.
Ecclesiastes

IN THE LAST chapter, I attempted to describe practical and tangible examples of how good can grow from grief. In the next few pages, I would like to take a more philosophical view while bearing in mind the possibility that a philosophical discourse may often raise as many questions as it answers. Even so, some questions seem too pressing to ignore.

Those who are mourning will at some point reflect about their own mortality and the meaning of their own life, as well as the life of their deceased loved one. When any of us face tragedy, we look for answers that are so hard to find, and as we mentioned earlier, they may never come to light. While many would counsel that all things in life work for the best, I suspect and suggest that while all things, even tragedy, can result in much good, all events in life may not necessarily be for the best.

For example, I could never see how crimes such as the Holocaust would ever be considered best in life for the victims or survivors, but some good could result if the survivors became advocates for other victims of modern day genocide attempts. The death of a child could not be considered best for a parent, but when people such as my grandparents take their tragedy and heavily invest their emotions and time in surviving children and grandchildren, good can appear. Much of the outcome depends on the person and upon their response to adverse events.

Even though we may ask why, rarely any answer satisfies or seems helpful. Neither speculation, philosophy, logic nor theology can completely ease the pain for most of us during the days, weeks or even months after an overwhelming loss. I don't wish to diminish the importance of our intellect or faith in dealing with tragedy, but rather to point out that the emotional weight of grief is so immense that even the strongest, the wisest and the most devout of us will struggle under the load. It is often devotion to our faith in God that gives us hope that just as our bodies heal, our souls do as well.

Frequent questions arise: if we are indeed created by an omnipotent and loving God, then why is there suffering and pain in this world? Why does grief happen and why is it so painful? Why does betrayal occur? Why does tragedy strike mankind? Why are there wars and genocidal campaigns?

I believe one of the reasons is because God gave mankind the ability to choose how to treat others. Otherwise, what is the joy in being loved, cherished and respected unless it is done out of free will rather than out of compulsion? Certainly we feel more loved by our spouses, parents, children and friends when they do it out of choice than when being forced to love us. And with that choice of free will come the results of choosing good things as well as from choosing those things which are out of the good graces of God.

Many of our circumstances are strongly influenced by those around us and their decisions. Good decisions do not always seem to prevail. The choices of other individuals (including former generations) affect not only their world, but our world and our lives as well.

And how do we assimilate the fact that human suffering and pain may occur today simply because of what happened many years ago? By accepting the fact that things we do this day can have effect on those who live dozens, hundreds or thousands of years after us. No doubt, the way we care for our community, our society and even our planet will affect others who live here after us.

The manner in which we treat our spouses will affect their lives for great good or great pain. The way we rear and educate our children will have either good or undesirable results for many generations to come. In a similar fashion, we are to some extent a product of the past. Of course, this does not absolve us from responsibility for the decisions we make in our own lives.

I believe in a loving God, and I believe there are forces of evil. But it seems that mankind bears much blame for many of life's misfortunes. Our free will allows us the choice of war or peace and the option of sharing or hoarding our resources, our food production and our wealth, the choice of whether or not we see to the health and material needs of the less fortunate. The choices of loyalty, honesty, generosity and fairness affect all our relationships.

History repeatedly records atrocities man has inflicted upon his fellow man; some even done under the guises of religion. Even today we find examples of crimes that mankind commits against mankind both on a local, national and international scale, often still done for religious as well as financial purposes. Even the institution of slavery still exists in many countries of the world to this day.

Often it is tempting to blame God for the hardships in life, when in reality we should attribute blame for many, if not most, difficulties in our world elsewhere. It is during times of suffering and grieving that faith in goodness, faith in friendships and faith in God gives us the strength to continue on with our lives.

I do not suppose to comprehend the ultimate reasons for life's hardships and tragedy. But I do believe in a benevolent God who cares deeply for us, hurts with us, gives us the strength to bear our grief, hears our prayers for comfort and will one day rectify the unfairness and pains of life. Faith, friends and even time itself seems to contain the gift of healing which begins during our mortal lives.

While grief takes much from us, it surprisingly gives us something in return - the opportunity to reflect upon our own lives and the compelling impetus to take advantage of our brief time here on earth. It is a time of commitment to do the good things in life that will make it a better place for others today and in the future. It is a time of deciding what is important in life. It is a time to commit to being a positive force on those within our sphere of influence.

Grief should not be viewed as a wasted episode in life. When we respond to it as best as we can, we can use our grief to remind ourselves of the temporality of mortal existence and to number our days in an effort to better serve our friends and neighbors – and perhaps mend some relationships with any estranged ones.

Life changes radically after the death of a loved one or the loss of love. There is no way to avoid the transformation. And we must change as well in order to go on with our lives. We must adjust our thoughts and hearts to live without the person or the relationship we lost. As we do so, we can change to become stronger and better people, those who do good things for others sooner rather than later, those who make the most of this short life as we try make a better world for others and ourselves. I believe we also prepare ourselves for a better world to come in the hereafter - a world with the hope of seeing our loved ones again and perhaps of finding some of the answers to the questions which we cannot find here on earth.

Understanding your tragedy may not be a reasonable goal. But understanding your response is a noble one. Our reaction to grief may seem uncontrollable at first, but as time flows we do have the opportunity to navigate our response. It is the voluntary –even compulsory- effort at healing and becoming a better person that determines the outcome of grief. The cause for grief is usually beyond our control. The response may be the only aspect over which we can have power.

If there is a key to surviving grief, it is an individual one which unlocks the door to recovery in ways unique to each person. Others may have a similar key, but you must discover your own. Frequently, it is in looking back that we realize we have found it.

The journey of grief is never one embarked upon voluntarily. It is one you are traveling reluctantly and with more emotional baggage than you wish to carry. Unlikely will it be a brief trip. At times you will feel as if it is an eternal passage.

Take encouragement from the stories you have read by those who have traveled this same road - and in fact are still making the journey of mourning. It is their and my desire that you not lose hope of better days ahead - days that await you after you have traveled this difficult path. Don't be surprised if you have some good days along the way.

One of many lessons I have learned from mourners is that some of the greatest deeds in life go beyond our status in society, our educational degrees and our material successes. For most of us, our greatest accomplishments will be our emotional support and relational investments in our family, friends and acquaintances. Grief serves as a profound reminder of the importance of those relationships and of our limited time in life to nurture them.

The pain of mourning will someday ease. The burden will slowly become lighter. The days will become brighter, and you *will* survive. And not only will you survive, but one day you will thrive! Impossible it may seem, but indeed it can happen. When it does, you will undoubtedly be an inspiration to others. For you, may that day come soon.

Resources

Listed below are resources for grief support.

American Association for Retired Persons (AARP)
601 E Street, NW
Washington, D.C. 20049
202-434-2260
www/aarp.org/griefandloss

Association for Death and Education and Counseling
324 North Main Street
West Hartford, CT 06117-2507
860-586-7503

Hospice Foundation of America
2001 S Street, NW, #300
Washington, D.C. 20009
202-638-5419
www.hospicefoundation.org

Miscarriage Support Auckland, Inc.
www.miscarriagesupport.org

Society of Military Widows
5535 Hempstead Way
Springfield, VA 22151
703-750-1342
www.militarywidows.org

SAVE Suicide Awareness Voices of Education
www.save.org

Website content and reliability is the responsibility of the sponsoring organization and not the author or publisher.

NOTES

American Psychiatric Association, *Diagnostic and Statistical Manual of Mental Disorders.* Washington, D.C.: American Psychiatric Association.

Lewis, C.S. *A Grief Observed.* San Francisco: Harper Collins. 2001.

Miscarriage Support Auckland, Inc. http://www.miscarriagesupport. org.nz/grief_issues.html. ©2006. Updated June 2007.

Maciejewski, Paul K. *An Empirical Examination of the Stage Theory of Grief.* Journal of the American Medical Association, 2007. 297: 716-723.

Rando, Theresa A. *Treatment of Complicated Mourning.* Champaign, IL: Research Press. 1993.

Shapiro, Ester R. *Grief As a Family Process.* New York: The Guilford Press. 1994.

Wolfelt, Alan D. *Death and Grief: A Guide for Clergy.* Muncie, IN: Accelerated Development Inc., Publishers. 1988.

D. KEITH COBB, M.D.

is an Internal Medicine physician
in practice near Savannah, Georgia.
He is a Clinical Assistant Professor of Medicine for The Medical
College of Georgia and Mercer University School of Medicine.
His office serves as a teaching site for medical students and resi-
dents from these institutions.

Dr. Cobb is a medical course writer for ArcMesa
Educators as well as a contributing writer and reviewer for the medical journal *Consultant* and
serves as GHC Hospice Medical Director, Savannah, GA.

D. Keith Cobb, M.D.
89 Interchange Drive
Richmond Hill, GA 31324

www.thegriefsurvivalhandbook.com

Unless otherwise noted, all opinions herein expressed are solely of the author.

Printed in the United States
By Bookmasters